Sailing in Windy Weather

Sailing in Windy Weather

The Seamanship Series

Richard Henderson

International Marine Publishing Company
Camden, Maine 04843

Published by International Marine Publishing Co.,
  a division of Highmark Publishing Ltd.,
  21 Elm Street, Camden, Maine 04843.

Typeset by Camden Type 'n Graphics, Camden, ME
Printed and bound by Bookcrafters, Chelsea, MI

10 9 8 7 6 5 4 3 2 1

Cynthia Bourgeault, Kathy Brandes, Editors
Janet Robbins, Production Coordinator

Library of Congress Cataloging-in-Publication Data

Henderson, Richard 1924–
  Sailing in windy weather.

  Bibliography: p.
  Includes index.
  1. Sailing. 2. Navigation. 3. Winds. I. Title.
GV811.5.H468 1988   797.1'24   87-22652
ISBN 0-87742-235-4

To my Son-in-law
Mark Cramer—
a great winch cranker and
all-around good seaman

Contents

1

Defining and Predicting Windy Weather

An old salt once remarked, "Nothing is more exasperating than trying to sail in a calm—a howling gale is preferable." Many modern sailors will agree, but a surprising number, particularly those who are new to the game, seem to have a deeply rooted fear of sailing in a decent breeze o' wind. They would much rather be drifting peacefully in a near calm. Of course, a certain amount of apprehension in a blow is healthy and a necessary ingredient of successful seamanship—it ensures foresight and caution. But real fear breeds panic, destroys judgment, causes undue stress, and, at the very least, takes the fun out of a good sail. In this book I will attempt to alleviate some of this fear of sailing in windy weather, but I won't do so by claiming that there are no potential dangers. Indeed, you can get into plenty of trouble with an unsuitable boat, lack of preparation, and poor seamanship. On the other hand, when you understand what to expect from the weather, have a well-equipped boat, and know how to handle her, the experience is utterly rewarding. There is nothing comparable to the exhilaration of seeing your boat take off on a semiplane, surfing down following seas, or watching and feeling her drive to windward with the spray flying—her well-shaped sails taut and straining. There is a wonderful sense of speed, power, and fulfillment—a feeling that you are actually harnessing the incredible forces of nature.

──────────── How Much Is a Blow?

Since 1805, the sailor's standard designation for wind strength has been the Beaufort Scale, which classifies the wind speed on a scale ranging from Force 0, a dead calm, to Force 12, a hurricane. The original scale, conceived by Admiral Francis Beaufort, related wind force to the speed and reefed condition of a square-rigged man-of-war, but more recent versions describe the effects of the wind observed at sea, the effects observed on land, and the effects on fishing smacks. One version even includes a psychological scale. This classification equates Beaufort Force 5 with "delight" and Force 6 with "delight tinged with anxiety." It is inevitable that at some point on the Beaufort Scale there will be a transition from delight to anxiety, but this book will suggest means of extending the transition to higher wind velocities.

This book concentrates on the middle ranges of the Beaufort Scale—Forces 5 through 8, or 17 to 40 knots. Force 5 (17 to 21 knots) is where windy weather sailing really begins. Eighteen knots is the usual threshold for Small Craft Advisory Signals to be posted (see illustration on page 17), alerting mariners to sustained weather or sea conditions, either present or forecast, that might be hazardous to small craft. In Forces 6 and 7 (22 to 27 knots and 28 to 33 knots, respectively), and oftentimes even in Force 8 (34 to 40 knots), it is possible to carry working sails and make some progress to windward, though with ever-deepening reefs. Beyond that, at the upper ranges of the Beaufort Scale, we leave the realm of windy-weather sailing and enter the realm of survival tactics. These are largely beyond the scope of this book, although chapter 7 considers them briefly.

When it comes to appraising boat behavior and sail reduction, even the modern version of the Beaufort Scale, with its "effect on fishing smacks" (based on observations of old-time, heavy-displacement trawlers working along the coast of England), is not very realistic or useful for modern yachtsmen sailing smart-handling, lighter-displacement yachts. Therefore, I have attempted to update this aspect of the Beaufort Scale by

Beaufort Scale

Beaufort number or force	Wind speed (knots)	Description	Effects observed far from land	Effects on fishing smack	Effects observed on land
0	under 1	Calm	Sea like mirror.	Fishing smack becalmed.	Calm; smoke rises vertically.
1	1-3	Light air	Ripples with appearance of scales; no foam crests	Fishing smack just has steerage way.	Smoke drift indicates wind direction; vanes do not move.
2	4-6	Light breeze	Small wavelets; crests of glassy appearance, not breaking.	Wind fills the sails of smacks which then travel at about 1-2 miles per hour.	Wind felt on face; leaves rustle; vanes begin to move.
3	7-10	Gentle breeze	Large wavelets; crests begin to break; scattered whitecaps.	Smacks begin to careen and travel about 3-4 miles per hour.	Leaves, small twigs in constant motion; light flags extended.
4	11-16	Moderate breeze	Small waves, becoming longer; numerous whitecaps.	Good working breeze, smacks carry all canvas with good list.	Dust, leaves, and loose paper raised up; small branches move.
5	17-21	Fresh breeze	Moderate waves, taking longer form; many whitecaps; some spray.	Smacks shorten sail.	Small trees in leaf begin to sway.
6	22-27	Strong breeze	Larger waves forming; whitecaps everywhere; more spray.	Smacks have doubled reef in mainsail; care required when fishing.	Larger branches of trees in motion; whistling heard in wires.
7	28-33	Moderate gale	Sea heaps up; white foam from breaking waves begins to be blown in streaks.	Smacks remain in harbor and those at sea lie-to.	Whole trees in motion; resistance felt in walking against wind.
8	34-40	Fresh gale	Moderately high waves of greater length; edges of crests begin to break into spindrift; foam is blown in well-marked streaks.	All smacks make for harbor, if near.	Twigs and small branches broken off trees; progress generally impeded.
9	41-47	Strong gale	High waves; sea begins to roll; dense streaks of foam; spray may reduce visibility.		Slight structural damage occurs; slate blown from roofs.
10	48-55	Whole gale	Very high waves with overhanging crests; sea takes white appearance as foam is blown in very dense streaks; rolling is heavy and visibility reduced.		Seldom experienced on land; trees broken or uprooted; considerable structural damage occurs.
11	56-63	Storm	Exceptionally high waves; sea covered with white foam patches; visibility still more reduced.		Very rarely experienced on land; usually accompanied by widespread damage.
12	64 and over	Hurricane	Air filled with foam; sea completely white with driving spray; visibility greatly reduced.		Very rarely experienced on land; usually accompanied by widespread damage.

*Based on scale from *American Practical Navigator* by Nathaniel Bowditch.

Modified Beaufort Scale

Beaufort Force	Knots	Effects on Fast Cruising Sloop
0 calm	under 1	no steerageway
1 light air	1–3	good steerageway with light sails
2 light breeze	4–6	moderate heeling and bone-in-teeth beginning when beating with No. 1 genoa jib
3 gentle breeze	7–10	noticeable stern wave; rail one or two feet out with No.1 genoa
4 moderate breeze	11–16	rail down when beating with No. 1 heavy genoa; flatten sails
5 fresh breeze	17–21	change to No. 2 genoa and then a shallow reef in the mainsail
6 strong breeze	22–27	deeper reef in main, then a No. 3 genoa or large working jib
7 moderate gale	28–33	deep reef in main and No. 2 working jib or forestaysail if cutter-rigged
8 fresh gale	34–40	storm trysail or deepest-reefed main and No. 2 working jib or spitfire
9 strong gale	41–47	storm trysail and spitfire; seek shelter if possible
10 whole gale	48–55	heave-to under counteracting storm sails; lie ahull; anchor; scud under bare poles or spitfire

A modified Beaufort Scale showing the effects of a building breeze on a fast cruising sloop. Below: Realistic sail combinations. *Opposite:* The effects summarized.

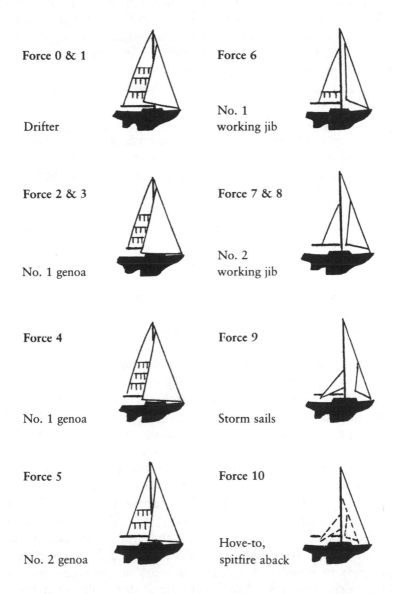

Force 0 & 1

Drifter

Force 6

No. 1
working jib

Force 2 & 3

No. 1 genoa

Force 7 & 8

No. 2
working jib

Force 4

No. 1 genoa

Force 9

Storm sails

Force 5

No. 2 genoa

Force 10

Hove-to,
spitfire aback

substituting a modern yacht for the fishing smack. Of course I can only generalize, because a boat's behavior depends on her size, her design, and other factors.

For the typical boat I have chosen a medium-sized (about 35 feet), fast, stiff, cruising sloop of conservative design. Such a boat would be a moderate-weight, deep-keeled racing-cruiser with modest sail area and keel ballast weighing a little more than 40 percent of her displacement. Her behavior and handling in different wind strengths are shown in the accompanying Beaufort Scale chart.

In Force 1, when the fishing smack is just getting steerageway, our racing-cruiser has good steerageway and handles quite smartly in three knots of wind with a large, lightweight jib. In Force 2, she definitely heels when beating with her largest jib (No. 1 genoa), and near six knots, a boat having a moderately full bow will begin to carry a "bone in her teeth" (or white foam at the bow). At Force 3, the stern wave begins to become quite noticeable (depending on the hull shape and weight of the boat), and she heels to a point where her rail is about one or two feet from the water (in the old days of wooden ships, they would say, "two or three planks out"). This depends, of course, on the boat's stiffness, or resistance to heeling. The rail might dip under water in the upper velocities of a Force 4 breeze, and then it is necessary to optimize the shapes of the sails by flattening the draft and moving it forward and adjusting the sheet leads. (More about this appears in chapter 5.) When the wind increases to Force 5, or just under that in a smaller boat, we would change to a smaller No. 2 genoa jib and begin reefing the mainsail. At Force 6, we would put in a deeper reef and then change to a No. 3 genoa or large working jib. A racer might carry a blast jib, a long-luff sail with no overlap. Force 7 would require a still-deeper reef and a No. 2 (small) working jib, while a cutter at this point would have her jib removed or furled and carry her forestaysail. Most well-equipped cruisers of the size and type under discussion would go to storm sails in a Force 8 gale, but to achieve progress to windward, the No. 2 working jib might supply better drive than a spitfire (a very small storm jib or staysail).

In a Force 9 gale, a boat of this size and type would be overburdened carrying more than a storm trysail and a spitfire. It is wise at this point to seek shelter if possible. Force 10 or above may call for storm tactics such as heaving-to, scudding, lying ahull, or other alternatives (chapter 7). The above effects on a fast cruising sloop will also be influenced by several factors other than the boat's exact size and design. For example, a great deal depends on the number, skill, and physical condition of the crew. Much depends, too, on whether or not the boat is being raced, for a boat usually will be driven harder and carry more sail during competition. For our purposes here, I am assuming that the boat is not being raced with a large crew but that she is being sailed at near-maximum efficiency. If the crew is small, seasick, or exhausted, then the sail reduction suggested would take place sooner, and the boat could be made to jog along at a more comfortable pace.

Predicting a Blow

It's a Force 5 day: a gusty southwester kicking up the whitecaps. But will the wind taper off by late afternoon, or will it gain strength as a storm moves in? In order to be able to anticipate potential dangers, every sailor should know what causes the wind to blow and should understand the basics of meteorology.

In the simplest terms, wind is caused by differences in atmospheric pressure, mainly as a result of temperature disparities; its horizontal direction is influenced also by the earth's rotation. High and low pressure systems march across the country in a generally west-to-east direction, although their exact paths are influenced by jetstream steering currents far aloft. Lows (also called cyclones or depressions), in which the atmospheric pressure is low, usually are associated with bad weather. They are atmospheric sinkholes into which the wind pours in an attempt to fill the void. In contrast, highs are mounds of air that force the wind out and downward. Just as

These photos, taken offshore from a Canadian meteorological vessel, illustrate wind and sea conditions throughout the middle range of the Beaufort Scale: Forces 5–8. (Courtesy U.S. Naval Institute)

Force 5 (17–21 knots). Moderate waves are taking a pronounced long form. Many whitecaps appear, with a chance of some spray.

Force 6 (22–27 knots). Large waves begin to form; the white foam crests are more extensive everywhere, and spray is likely.

Force 7 (28—33 knots). The sea heaps up, and white foam from breaking waves begins to be blown in streaks along the direction of the wind.

Force 8 (34–40 knots). The moderately high waves are of greater length, and the edges of the crests begin to break into spindrift. The foam is blown in well-marked streaks along the direction of the wind.

water seeks its own level, the air pressure seeks equilibrium, causing the wind to move away from a high and toward a low.

A complicating factor in all this is the Coriolis force. Because of the earth's rotation, this force deflects the wind (or other moving object) to the right in the Northern Hemisphere and to the left in the Southern Hemisphere. As a result, the wind flows in a clockwise direction around and away from a Northern Hemisphere high and flows into and counterclockwise around a low. In accordance with Buys Ballot's Law, you can locate pressure cells if you stand with your back to the gradient (general) wind and then turn about 25 degrees to the right. In the Northern Hemisphere, low pressure will be on your left side and higher pressure on your right. (Gradient wind does not include such factors as local conditions, the funneling of wind down a river valley, or suction effects from a sun-heated shore.)

A barometer gauges atmospheric pressure, and every sailor should use one of these valuable instruments. Changes in wind velocity and direction often can be forecast by observing rises and falls of pressure. The sailor's barometer (often called a "glass") is the aneroid type—a small, round box with a vacuum chamber having thin, corrugated surfaces that are bent by pressure changes. These changes are transmitted mechanically to an index pointer, and they are noted by comparing the pointer to a setting hand directly above it. This hand must be set and read periodically. It is not enough merely to know what the barometer reads at a given moment; you must know what the pressure is doing—whether it is rising or falling and how rapidly. This information is then correlated with wind direction and observations of the sky to give some idea of future weather.

Be cautious when there is a quick rise in pressure, and especially when there is a steady rapid fall, as strong winds may follow. When the glass is falling well below 30 inches, particularly when easterly winds are backing (shifting counterclockwise), look out for stormy weather. Ancient doggerel proclaims, "At sea with low and falling glass, soundly sleeps a careless ass." In contrast, a steady high glass indicates that a high is sitting over you and that fair weather will continue, but winds are apt to be exasperatingly light.

Closely associated with low-pressure cells are weather fronts, which are boundaries between air masses of different temperature and moisture content. This boundary is called a cold front when a cold mass advances against warmer air and a warm front when a warm mass advances against colder air. A front passing through produces a change in the weather, and usually the wind veers, i.e., shifts in a clockwise direction. Very often, a cold front will produce strong winds, especially if a squall line (line of dark, stormy clouds) precedes it. Lows may form along a stationary front as a result of a cyclonic wave or kink that develops from friction produced by opposing winds on each side of the front. This forms a frontal V with a low at the point of the V and a warm and cold front on each leg of the V. The accompanying diagram depicts the birth and decay of an extratropical low as it might evolve in the Northern Hemisphere. Notice that the leading warm front is overtaken by the faster-moving cold front to form an occlusion when the cool air ahead of the warm front and the cold air behind the cold front meet and force the warm air aloft. Regardless of how the low decays, the illustration shows why the passage of a warm front often is followed closely by the passage of a cold front.

Although lows are most often associated with stormy weather, strong winds can occur after the passage of a cold front when the sky is clearing and the barometer is rising. An old weather adage warns, "Quick rise after low portends a stronger blow." This is a common occurrence, so be prepared for it. A blow also may occur when a high overtakes a low and the two systems reinforce each other to produce a strong gradient wind between the two pressure cells. On the other hand, a stationary high may merely block an approaching low. Study an up-to-date weather map, bearing in mind that when isobars (lines connecting equal points of pressure) are close together, the winds will be strong. In contrast, the middle area between two highs or two lows, known by meteorologists as a "col," is a region of light airs.

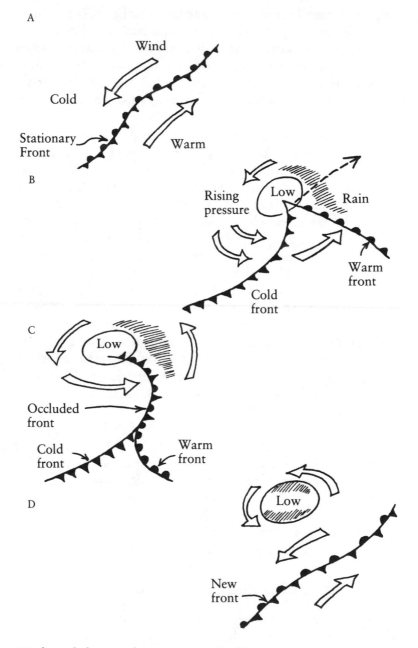

Birth and decay of an extratropical low.

Clouds are the most apparent harbingers of weather, and the main types are shown in the accompanying illustration. Generally speaking, the upper clouds—the "mares' tails and

CIRROCUMULUS "mackerel sky" (over 20,000 ft.) can predict approach of warm front in unstable air

CIRRUS "mares' tails" (over 25,000 ft.) if thick often advanced forerunners (24 hours or more) ahead of a front

ALTOSTRATUS (about 19,000 ft.) gray sheet often warns of approaching warm front

CIRROSTRATUS (over 20,000 ft.) whitish sheet often causing halo around sun—can warn of approaching warm front

CUMULONIMBUS "thunderhead" (thunderstorm cloud—can reach height of cirrus

ALTOCUMULUS (over 12,000 ft.) like sheet— can warn nof colf front in unstable air

STRATOCUMULUS (about 8,000 ft.) dark globular rolls

CUMULUS (over 4,000 ft.) fair weather unless extreme towering up

NIMBOSTRATUS (about 3,000 ft.) dark rain cloud

STRATUS (about 1,500 ft.) gray sheet

Clouds. (Courtesy Contemporary Books)

mackerel sky" that "make tall ships carry small sails"—are forerunners of an approaching front. They do not predict imminent bad weather, but when the sky begins to thicken with middle-altitude and lower clouds, the weather could deteriorate in the near future. Sheet, or foglike, altostratus clouds are a particularly reliable indicator of bad weather to come. On the other hand, lower stratocumulus clouds, which form from deteriorating cumulus, normally indicate fair weather. Puffy cumulus are fair-weather clouds, unless they rear up exceedingly high on a hot and humid day and grow dark near their base. Then they have turned into cumulonimbus (thunderstorm) clouds, which can bring a short-lived storm with strong, shifty winds. Fair-weather cumulus along the shore might indicate the coming of a seabreeze, as a result of hot air rising over the land and sucking in cooler air from above the water.

If the weather system wind is blowing onshore, it could be reinforced sufficiently by the seabreeze to produce a fresh wind requiring sail reduction. Even a light upper-gradient wind that

Basic principle of the seabreeze.

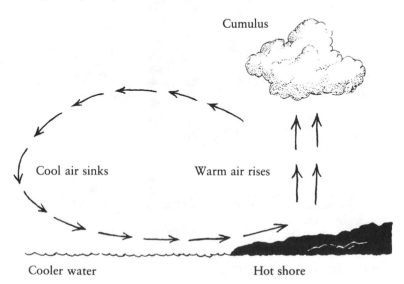

Cumulus

Cool air sinks   Warm air rises

Cooler water   Hot shore

opposes the seabreeze can create conditions that encourage a stronger surface wind from the water. There is evidence that a fresh seabreeze will block an isolated thunderstorm that forms over the land.

If there is a weather warning display site in your vicinity, by all means obey its signals, displayed by pennants or flags in the daytime and by lights at night. A well-found cruising boat with an experienced crew often can venture out in relative safety when the Small Craft Advisory signal is posted. The Gale Warning usually calls for storm sails, and the more prudent course is to remain in port. No need to say that you should stay home when the latter two signals are displayed.

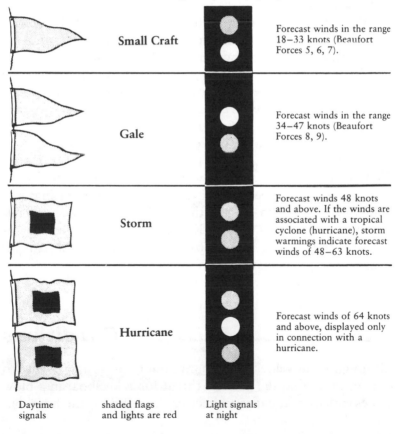

Small Craft		Forecast winds in the range 18–33 knots (Beaufort Forces 5, 6, 7).
Gale		Forecast winds in the range 34–47 knots (Beaufort Forces 8, 9).
Storm		Forecast winds 48 knots and above. If the winds are associated with a tropical cyclone (hurricane), storm warmings indicate forecast winds of 48–63 knots.
Hurricane		Forecast winds of 64 knots and above, displayed only in connection with a hurricane.

| Daytime signals | shaded flags and lights are red | Light signals at night |

What has been said thus far only touches on the rudiments of meteorology. Before you leave home to go sailing, listen to forecasts on the radio and or television. Particularly helpful are the NOAA VHF/FM broadcasts on seven high-band frequencies ranging from 162.400 to 162.550 mHz, updated every two to three hours in many areas. A weather map on TV gives you a good idea of how the general weather pattern is developing. You can see if a low-pressure system or front is approaching and judge the wind strength by the closeness of the isobars (when they are shown).

The U.S. Department of Commerce issues NOAA *Marine Weather Service Charts* for most coastal areas. These charts show the locations of weather-warning displays, the location and range of VHF/FM radio stations, and other useful information.

Valuable as these aids may be, however, every sailor should make his or her own meteorological observations by studying the barometer, the sky, and the wind directions. This is important because weather bureau reports are broad in scope, and conditions can be altered by local effects, such as the geography of a particular area. Very often the report will be basically correct, but a forecast change might arrive earlier or later than predicted, or the wind might blow with more or less force than expected. There is nothing like on-the-spot observations. Weather phenomena are repetitious, so it is very helpful for a neophyte sailor to keep a log, even just shorthand jottings in a notebook or diary, to describe the wind, seas, clouds, barometric pressure, and even the tide. Knowing what to expect weatherwise may help you avoid getting caught in a wind stronger than you or your boat can handle.

Sea Conditions

Although wind velocity is of paramount concern, it is wise to bear in mind that the greatest threat for a keelboat in a blow comes not from the direct effect of the wind on the boat, but

Sea State Table		
Beaufort Force	Description and wave heights	Sea state
0, 1	Calm glassy 0	0
2	Rippled 0 to $1/3$ foot	1
3	Smooth $1/3$ to $1 2/3$ feet	2
4	Slight 2 to 4 feet	3
5	Moderate 4 to 8 feet	4
6	Rough 8 to 13 feet	5
7, 8, 9	Very rough 13 to 20 feet	6
10	High 20 to 30 feet	7
11	Very high 30 to 45 feet	8
12	Phenomenal over 45 feet	9

from the wind's effect on the water, making seas. For this there is a Sea State Code, which *The American Practical Navigator* (generally referred to as "Bowditch," the author's last name) relates to the Beaufort Scale. The code, reproduced here, is useful, but it has severe limitations. Whether or not the seas are dangerous depends on their character and not necessarily their height. To determine the character of the seas, you need to know at least five facts: the wind velocity, its duration, the length of fetch, the water depth, and the state of the current. The duration is the length of time the wind has been blowing

Wave Characteristics

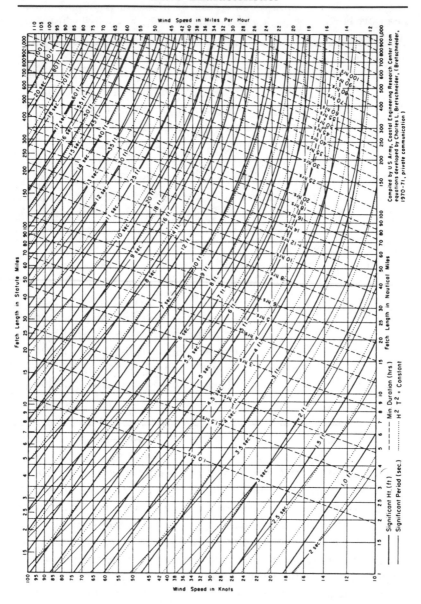

Wave characteristics as a function of wind speed, fetch, and duration.

from the same direction. In general, the longer the duration the higher the seas, although the rate of increase in height slows progressively as time increases. Then, too, a severe windshift can produce extremely confused seas where the wave lines cross and cause peaked-up crests. Fetch is the distance from a windward shore or, at sea, the distance from the wind's point of origin (such as the edge of a storm). The greater the distance the higher the seas, but again, the rate of increase diminishes as fetch increases. Usually, when you tuck up under a windward shore, you get into a lee and the seas are much smoother. (Do not be confused by the term *lee shore*. A popular boating writer erroneously advised heading for "the protection of a lee shore," and even Webster of dictionary fame was mistaken about the term. A lee shore is the shore onto which the wind is blowing, and that is what you want to avoid. During a blow seek the windward shore for protection.)

The accompanying graph, prepared by oceanographer Charles Bretschneider, shows the influence of wind speed, duration, and fetch on wave height and period. (Wave period is the time in seconds between the passing of two successive wave crests over a fixed point.) Duration and fetch are limiting factors that prevent seas from becoming fully developed. For example, a 40-knot wind would have to blow for 42 hours over a 710-mile fetch to produce a 30-foot sea. Fortunately for sailors, waves seldom are fully developed in the upper wind velocities, even in midocean.

Major influences on the character of the seas are the current and the water depth. A current flowing against the wind can produce steep, choppy, and often confused seas. Shallow water also produces choppy seas, which are more likely to have breaking crests. Unless you are seeking shelter close under a shore, it is often better to stay in the deepest water for smoother seas. An exception to this advice could be when the deep water, particularly in a channel, produces a strong flow of current against the wind. Keep in mind that the current is usually strongest and slowest to change in deep water.

2

The Boat's Behavior in Windy Weather

The fundamental prerequisite for the enjoyment of sailing in strong winds is having a suitable boat whose behavior you understand. If you do not have a seagoing boat, you must know her limitations and allow an ample margin of safety. My most frightening experience aboard a boat was during a sail in a mere Force 5 breeze. Another time, during a Force 10 gale at sea, I was relatively relaxed. The different reactions were due to the boats and their equipment. In the first-mentioned instance, the boat—newly acquired by a friend with limited sailing experience—was a home-built, home-designed West Indian sloop with an open cockpit and no flotation. I soon discovered that she had a strong weather helm on one tack but a lee helm on the other tack, and it was then that my friend told me his bargain boat had a cracked keel. Soon after this, I learned that there was neither a bilge pump nor any provision for bailing. By this time, we were out of the harbor and in the full force of the tradewinds, with no land to leeward. Realizing we had to beat back and should do so at once, I suggested that we try to bring the sloop about. We turned her into the wind, but she missed stays. After she gained sternway, I reversed the helm and backed the jib, but she simply would not change tacks. After several more tries, I realized we would have to jibe around. One mistake and we'd have been in the drink, with little if any chance of being rescued. But we jibed successfully and eventually reached the harbor again. There, as tactfully as possible, I suggested that my friend get rid of his boat or at least keep her restricted to sheltered waters.

In the midst of the Force 10 gale during a transatlantic passage, I admit to a feeling of some apprehension, but there was no real fear, because I had confidence in our 37-footer, *Kelpie*, and her gear. (That confidence was reinforced when I later heard that a sister boat went through the disastrous 1979 Fastnet Race storm with the only damage, according to her skipper, amounting to "approximately one dollar and twenty-five cents for a new sail batten and a whistle for the kettle.") We had tested her for a year before going offshore and had spent much of that time modifying her and acquiring proper gear, including small storm sails. That gale was far from pleasant, and I would not like to go through it again, but having confidence in the boat made all the difference between a horrible experience and one that was merely uncomfortable. It was even fascinating at times.

Boat Types

Although it is not necessary to have a rugged offshore vessel to enjoy sailing in fresh winds, you certainly should have some idea of your boat's capabilities. Although oceans have been crossed by open canoes, dories, and other cockleshells, more than a few sailors have been lost in such craft. It is unquestionably most prudent to limit a boat's use to the purpose for which she was designed.

In order to classify the various types of sailboats, I am listing them as follows: sailboards, dinghies, daysailers, overnighters, cruising-racers, racing-cruisers, and offshore cruisers. Of course, there is some overlapping of types, but at least this classification provides a means by which the different kinds of boats can be brought into a discussion.

Sailboards

A sailboard has a surfboardlike hull, with no cockpit and very low freeboard. I won't discuss sailing these craft, because this book really is about sailing *vessels*, but I must say that it is remarkable what strong winds some of these boats can take. I have seen expert sailboarders standing on their boards, darting to and fro with apparent ease, while large craft were struggling along under reefed sails. Nevertheless, sailboarding (or wind-gliding) is a sport with greater accent on balance and athletic ability than on seamanship, and it is a form of sailing that should be practiced close to shore and near readily available rescue facilities. Even very skilled sailboarders should figure on spending a fair amount of time in the drink. When the water is

Although not technically a sailing vessel, *a sailboard will stand up to remarkably strong winds. (Lachlan Clarke photo)*

cold, it is essential to have a wet suit, dry suit, or similar garb designed to hold in the body's heat.

The same general constraints apply to those enormously popular hybrids, the Sunfish (and other boats of the Sunfish type). Midway between sailboard and sailing dinghy, these tiny craft can deliver a good deal of sailing pleasure and encourage the development of sailing skills. But their very low freeboard and shallow, footwell-type cockpits make them most suitable for sheltered waters.

Sailing Dinghies

For the sake of this discussion, a sailing dinghy is a small, open, centerboard boat having considerably more freeboard than a sailboard and also having gunwales (or at least lacking very wide side decking). It is important to realize that this type of boat cannot be allowed to heel to the point where water flows over her leeward gunwale. If this happens the boat can fill and swamp or capsize. The skipper and crew must hike out or put their weight far to windward to prevent excessive heeling. Most modern dinghies do have at least some side decking—quite often it is rolled or curved for comfortable hiking. Such boats usually are fitted with a lot of flotation that often is placed low under the side decks to help resist knockdowns and, of course, to prevent sinking in the event of a capsize. The tradeoff for this kind of flotation, however, is that it may encourage the boat to turn turtle (upside-down), making the boat more difficult to right. If the water is shallow, the masthead could become stuck in a muddy bottom. Sometimes masthead flotation is fitted to prevent turtling after a capsize, but this will cause a boat lying on her side to present a lot of area to the wind and make her blow off to leeward, possibly away from her crew if they should happen to become separated from the boat. Chapter 6 covers the handling of these boats, but here it is necessary only to recommend some limitations on their use.

Although a few dinghies, such as the Wayfarer, have made successful trips far offshore, an ocean passage in an open boat without a cabin and with limited supplies generally falls in the

The 12-foot Tech Dinghy, designed by Halsey Herreshoff. Note the lack of side decking, typical of an open dinghy. A boat of this type can swamp or capsize if allowed to heel to a point where her leeward gunwale goes under. (Courtesy Harken-Vanguard)

category of a stunt. I would never recommend taking an easily capsizable boat into unprotected waters. Dinghies are designed for sheltered or semisheltered bays, lakes, harbors, or rivers. They can go cautiously into exposed waters in fair weather, but no boat of this type should be sailed such a distance from shore that it cannot return to shelter within an hour or so. It is the safest policy not to take a dinghy out in a strong wind when the weather is cold and there are no rescue facilities nearby. This is particularly true when the boat has little flotation and low freeboard and holds a lot of water in the swamped condition. If she also has a partially open centerboard well that is low, she will be extremely difficult to bail out, especially in choppy sea conditions. On the other hand, many modern dinghies are self-rescuing—i.e., they are easy to right after a capsize, float high when swamped, and have suction bailers or automatic drainage with the boat moving. Such craft can be taken farther out in fresh winds when the weather is warm and the crew experienced.

Daysailers

My idea of a daysailer is a family boat somewhat larger than a dinghy that has wider side decking. She can be heeled a bit farther than a dinghy without shipping water, although the degree of allowable heel may depend on whether she has a centerboard or a keel. The latter type generally is more seaworthy, as it capsizes less easily. Many daysailers are open boats, however, so any water that enters the cockpit will find its way into the bilge. Thus, a keelboat of this type should be fitted with flotation to prevent sinking in the event of a severe knockdown. Any sinkable boat with an open cockpit must be fitted with sufficient flotation to keep her afloat under any circumstances. (More about this later.) The sailing range of an open daysailer, whether centerboarder or keelboat, should not be a great deal more than a dinghy's, but a sailor of moderate skill might be able to take her out in relatively stronger winds because of her greater resistance to capsize. Keep in mind, however, that self-rescue might be more difficult in the larger daysailer, so great care is crucial in a real blow. The fastest boats of this type—as well as those in the dinghy category that are intended for the most competitive kind of racing—can be quite tricky to sail in a fresh breeze. They are best handled by experts when the wind is really piping. A plus, however, is that this kind of boat is high in dynamic stability. In other words, she gains stability at reasonably fast speeds when kept flat.

Overnighters

An overnighter has a small cabin and usually can be made watertight. When this is the case, the cockpit is self-draining,

The legendary O'Day Day Sailer, designed by Uffa Fox. With wider side decking than a dinghy, daysailers have greater resistance to capsizing. Even so, a centerboard or open daysailer should not be sailed far from sheltered waters—and probably not in wind conditions beyond Force 6. (Courtesy Lear Siegler Marine)

and there are hatches that can be closed to keep the water out under any conditions. When such a boat has respectable stability, she can be very safe almost anywhere when handled by an experienced seaman. Indeed, one of the smallest boats of this type, the 15-foot West Wight Potter, has made remarkable

Small, but sturdy and seaworthy, the 15-foot West Wight Potter has made remarkable long distance offshore passages. (Courtesy HMS Marine)

long-distance offshore passages, although I myself would not recommend anything this small for crossing oceans. Some overnighters such as the Potter have not only watertight integrity but also flotation, which adds an extra measure of safety. The most important criteria of seaworthiness, however, relate to such matters as strength of construction, soundness of rig and gear, good handling characteristics, and stability. These matters vary with different boats and must be appraised individually. Before taking any overnighter far offshore, I would subject her to ample trials in rough weather and practice handling her in all conditions.

Cruising-Racers and Racing-Cruisers

A distinction should be made between a cruising-racer and a racing-cruiser. The former is primarily a racing boat with limited cruising accommodations, while the latter is first and foremost a cruiser, but a fast one that can be raced. Both types

Cruising-racer versus racing-cruiser.

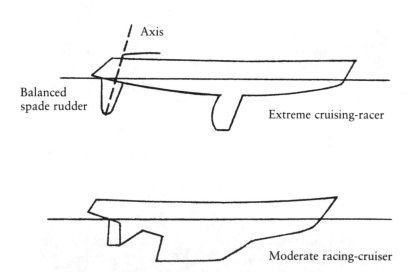

can be amply seaworthy and might be taken anywhere in almost any kind of weather, but again, this depends on the individual boat. Some of the extreme cruising-racers of very light displacement with extrawide beam, flattish bottoms, high centers of gravity, and tall, flimsy rigs have proven vulnerable or at least hard to handle in a blow at sea, even when they were designed to compete under offshore handicap rules. On the other hand, a moderate design, probably more often seen in the racing-cruiser category, is more likely to be a wholesome boat that will be trouble-free in a hard chance offshore.

Such a boat should have enough displacement to ensure robust construction and reasonable momentum for good performance to windward with an easy motion in choppy seas. The displacement-length ratio (D/L) ought to be above 150 for a versatile, seaworthy cruising-racer and between 250 and 350 for a racing-cruiser. (These numbers are derived by dividing the boat's weight in tons by the cube of .01 times her waterline length.)

The conservative boat will have modest freeboard and beam. One rule-of-thumb for beam is that it be no more than a quarter of the waterline length plus three feet. Beam as well as ballast determines the boat's stability, and this important subject is covered in more detail later. In areas of predominant strong winds, it might be best for a cruising sailor to avoid the cruising-racer with an extremely short keel (short in the fore-and-aft direction), as this can lessen directional stability and make the helm overly sensitive. This is particularly true when the rudder is a balanced spade, having an entirely underwater blade detached from the keel or skeg and with its leading edge forward of its turning axis (see illustration). Such a helm must be handled very carefully every moment, especially in a fresh breeze.

Offshore Cruisers

In theory, offshore cruisers are the most seagoing boats, ones that can take almost any kind of heavy weather. They usually are fairly heavy, with a D/L of over 300, and they have fairly long keels to provide good directional stability and modest draft. In contrast to cruising-racers, which often have fine bows and full sterns, the offshore cruiser usually has more symmetrical lines, with the hull a bit narrower aft and slightly fuller forward. This characteristic helps provide steadiness on the helm when the boat is heeled, although too much symmetry

The Cabot 36, one example of a comfortable offshore cruiser.

can cause hobbyhorsing (excessive pitching) in a seaway. Perhaps the greatest drawback of some offshore cruisers is lack of speed and maneuverability, with mediocre windward ability. When displacement is too great and wetted surface area is high because of a very long keel, sailing ability suffers, and the rig then needs to be quite large to gain power in light airs. I would not be afraid to take a moderately heavy offshore cruiser anywhere, provided she was well built, had a strong and handy rig, and could sail well enough to beat away from a lee shore in a blow.

Boat Size

Size is an important consideration in regard to the seaworthiness of a vessel. How she fares in rough seas will depend to a large extent on the relativity of wave and boat size. A smaller boat might ride comfortably over a large wave that would violently rock or roll a larger vessel, but a slightly choppy sea that would not bother the larger boat could have a violent effect on the smaller craft. In most rough-weather conditions, the larger vessel has the advantage, although one hears occasional arguments to the contrary. She will less often encounter troublesome seas, and the scaling laws work in her favor. These laws, related to those used in model tank testing, indicate that the larger vessel has the advantage with regard to roll inertia, initial stability, and wind velocity. A smaller, geometrically similar sister boat feels a stronger wind for a given velocity, and she is more tender (heels more easily). This is one reason why designers give small boats greater proportional beam, although doing so may compromise the range of stability.

To avoid an unnecessarily complicated discussion, let me generalize with the admittedly simplistic statement that given two boats that are more or less equal except in size, the larger boat can be taken out in higher winds, rougher seas, and farther offshore. She usually is more stable and drier, pounds less, and can be driven to windward more easily than her smaller sister. Bear in mind, however, that size is only one element of seaworthiness, and a small boat may be easier to handle. Certainly there are plenty of small offshore cruisers that are more able than a variety of larger vessels that are not designed for offshore work.

——— Flotation and Watertightness

Another vital component of seaworthiness is watertightness, which can be achieved with good design, awareness of the boat's vulnerability, and the installation of flotation. As mentioned earlier, any sinkable boat with an open cockpit should have flotation. On two occasions I have seen racing daysailers sink in deep water after they were knocked down by strong puffs during squalls. These founderings were entirely unnecessary and could not have happened if the boats had been fitted with flotation. It doesn't take very much flotation to keep a small boat buoyant. A cubic foot of closed-cell plastic, which cannot absorb water, will buoy up from 50 to 62 pounds in fresh water. A small cruiser may need little more than foam filling in the space under two bunks. Then too, air tanks can double as limited stowage compartments when they have watertight doors, usually screw-in access ports.

Unsinkability is not a necessary requirement for a well-designed cabin cruiser with a self-bailing cockpit, but in the smaller sizes, at least, this type of boat should be fitted with flotation when it has vulnerable hatches or openings. Vulnerability can come from hatches that are too far to one side of the boat's centerline; hatches, ports, or windows that are difficult to close and lock; or a companionway opening with a very low sill.

A hatch far off the centerline is especially vulnerable during a so-called white squall—a strong, unexpected gust that occurs in fair weather. In foul weather, the hatch ordinarily would be closed, but in the rare instance of a white squall, the boat could be knocked down with her hatch open. If the opening is on the low side, serious downflooding could result. In contrast, a centerline hatch that is not excessively wide usually will stay out of the water during a knockdown on either tack. Opening windows and ports in the topsides are extremely vulnerable to flooding in knockdowns, and they should be kept closed whenever the boat is under sail. Some companionway sills are only a few inches above the sole (floor) of a self-bailing cockpit, and when this is the case, a dropboard or solid lock-in slide should be inserted in breezy weather, raising the sill at least to the level of the cockpit seats.

Stability

The threat of capsize is probably the greatest cause for fear of sailing in strong winds. There are some misconceptions about capsizing, so it is helpful to examine the basic physics of the phenomenon. A boat capsizes when her positive stability turns to negative—or, in other words, when she no longer can right herself automatically. Let's say she is heeled over by the wind or a wave until she lies on her beam ends, with her deck vertical or nearly so. If she self-rights (comes back upright automatically from this position), she has not actually capsized but only suffered a severe knockdown. Should she flop over and submerge her rig, however, then she has capsized, and if she continues to roll over bottom-side-up, she has turned turtle. The degree of heel at which a boat capsizes will depend on her range of positive stability, and the limit of that range occurs when the center of gravity (CG) of the heeled hull comes into vertical alignment with its center of buoyancy (CB). The latter is the center of the hull's underwater volume, representing the concentration of all forces keeping the boat afloat. It is on the boat's centerline when she is upright but moves progressively to leeward as she heels in the initial stages. On the other hand, the CG (the center of the boat's displacement and on-board weights) is fixed, so the two centers will vary in horizontal distance from each other as the boat changes her angle of heel. This relationship is evident in the accompanying illustration, which shows a centerboard boat capsizing. Notice that a righting moment is created by the separation of the two centers until the CG moves directly above the CB, the limit of the positive stability range. Any further heeling will result in a capsize. At this point of heel, or preferably before, the crew should have climbed onto the centerboard to move the CG to windward and thus create a righting moment. Of course, the

The basic physics of a capsize in a centerboarder. As the boat heels, the center of buoyance (CB) and center of gravity (CG) move farther apart, creating, in essence, a long lever arm that results in positive righting moment. At a high angle of heel, the two centers again move close together, until the CG moves directly above the CB, the limit of the positive stability range. Any further heeling will result in a capsize.

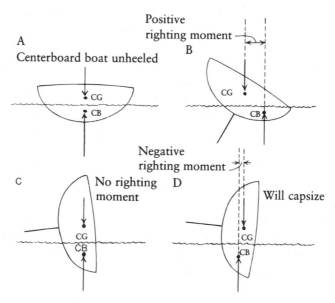

cautious skipper never deliberately allows his boat to approach the end of her stability range. Chapter 6 discusses the techniques for preventing such situations.

Generally speaking, keelboats have much greater stability ranges than centerboarders. In the illustration, the centerboarder will capsize at about 80 degrees of heel, but most dinghies with open cockpits will capsize before this—usually when their gunwales are submerged. The stability ranges of keelboats vary considerably, depending primarily on the cockpit design, the amount and location of ballast, and the boat's beam. Boats with the longest stability range have watertight decks (with self-bailing cockpits), ballast-displacement ratios (B/D) of 35 percent or more, and moderate-to-narrow beam. An example of an adequate stability range for offshore cruising appears in the accompanying illustration, which shows the stability curve for *Kelpie,* my racing-cruiser. Her

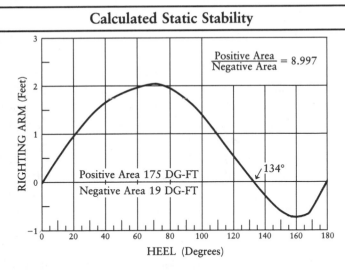

Stability curve for Kelpie, *an Ohlson 38A, as calculated under the IMS (International Measurement System). Above the base line the curve shows positive stability; below the line, negative stability. The ratio of positive to negative is shown in the upper right corner. (Courtesy USYRU)*

greatest resistance to capsize (maximum righting moment) occurs at 75 degrees of heel, and she will not capsize until reaching a heeling angle of 134 degrees (when her mast is sticking down in the water 44 degrees beyond horizontal). The curve under the baseline represents negative stability (stability in the inverted position).

An important calculation is the stability ratio, the ratio of area under the positive stability curve (above the baseline) to the area under the negative curve (below the baseline). *Kelpie*'s is just under 9 (the higher the number the better). The accompanying graph shows the stability ranges and ratios of boats racing under the IMS (International Measurement System). Most of these boats have stability ranges of 120 degrees and ratios of 4. For extensive offshore cruising or distance racing, I would not recommend boats with numbers lower than these. The stability numbers of most stock boats—at least those that have been measured under the IMS—can be obtained from the USYRU (United States Yacht Racing Union) or the IYRU (International Yacht Racing Union).

After the 1979 Fastnet Race, when a number of racing boats were knocked down in an unusually violent gale, studies were made to determine the design characteristics that encouraged capsizing. It was found, not surprisingly, that light-displacement, beamy boats with high centers of gravity were the most susceptible. A simple rule-of-thumb, called the Capsize Screening Formula, was developed by the USYRU's Safety-at-Sea Committee. To apply the formula, take the boat's beam in feet and divide that by the cube root of her displacement in cubic feet. To obtain the volume of water she displaces, divide her weight in pounds by 64 (the weight of a cubic foot of seawater). To pass the screening, the result should be 2 or lower. For example, *Kelpie* has a beam of 10¼ feet and a displacement of 15,000 pounds. Applying her figures to the formula gives:

$$\frac{10.25}{\sqrt[3]{\dfrac{15000}{64}}} = \frac{10.25}{\sqrt[3]{234.37}} = \frac{10.25}{6.1655} = 1.662$$

IMS Fleet Distributions of Stability Limit and Ratio

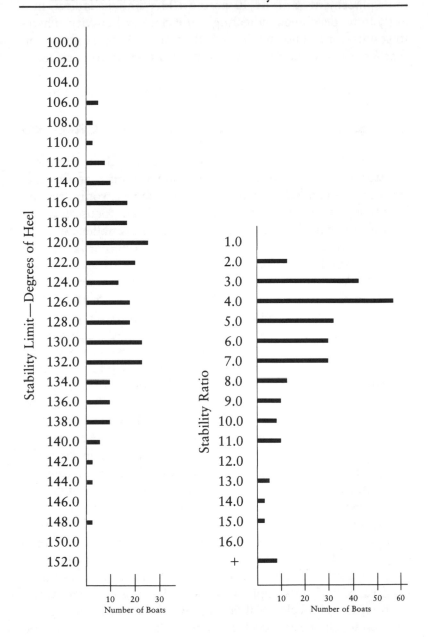

She passes the test with ease. Furthermore, *Kelpie* has a ballast-to-displacement ratio of 40 percent. Her ballast is low, in a fairly long, deep keel, indicating a low center of gravity. Therefore, without even seeing her stability curve, I can be confident that *Kelpie* is a relatively safe boat with respect to capsize.

Safety Features

Aside from the general hull shape, weight, ballast, flotation, and watertightness, there are some design details that are especially recommended for rough water. Of course, sound rigging is vital, as discussed in chapter 3, but here I will focus on major deck and cockpit details, beginning with the smaller boats.

It is definitely helpful when a dinghy or open daysailer has at least a small foredeck with a coaming to keep water out of the bilge. When there is no foredeck and the boat is open all the way forward, it is not a bad idea to have a removable fabric spray hood for protection when beating into choppy seas. Many low-freeboard boats, especially those with minimal flotation, need substantial washboards (protective strips on the foredeck), normally V-shaped and slightly canted forward, to deflect solid water. Decked-over daysailers with open cockpits should have side decking sufficiently wide to keep the water out if the boat should happen to submerge her rail or deck edge. I like to see a low coaming entirely around the cockpit on this type of boat. Not only does it help keep the cockpit dry, but it keeps the crew from slipping to leeward when they are sitting up on the windward deck. A stern deck is also a desirable safety feature to reduce the risk of shipping a following sea. If there is no stern deck, there should be self-bailers, transom flaps, or other openings to drain water from the cockpit. Dinghies often need hiking straps, under which the crew can put their feet in order to lean out as far as possible to windward, and thus apply maximum righting leverage, when the boat is well heeled. All decked-over boats large enough to have crew on the foredeck need toerails entirely around the deck edge or slightly inboard. These act as foot braces and help prevent the crew from slipping overboard. All decks should be skidproofed with either a molded-in, nonslip pattern, or adhesive deck tread, or abrasive paint. This is especially important when the deck has a high crown.

Larger boats with cabins and self-bailing cockpits need drains large enough to clear a filled cockpit well within two or three minutes at least. There should be seacocks on every drain where the drain hose attaches to the fitting that penetrates the hull. It is important that each through-hull fitting can be closed quickly and easily in case a hose happens to crack or slip off its fitting. Be sure there is an adequate means of clearing the bilge of water. Offshore boats should have two large-capacity, permanently installed bilge pumps—one that can be operated below decks and the other operable from the helm. I am partial to the diaphragm type with a removable handle. A necessary requirement for rough-weather sailing anywhere is dogs (latches) on hatches. These are sometimes lacking on cockpit seat locker lids, but during a knockdown, they can prevent the lids from falling open.

I have already mentioned the importance of a high companionway sill and/or a dropboard to close at least the lower part of the vertical opening. An accompanying caveat is that when the sides of the companionway opening slant away from the vertical, a very slight lifting of the dropboard will detach it from the side grooves into which it fits. Therefore, the board must be locked into place to prevent it from falling out during a knockdown. You can do this with a simple slide bolt, but a better system for closing the whole opening is the so-called Fastnet storm-slide arrangement, which is required on some ocean racers. As can be seen in the accompanying photographs, when the dropboard's handle is turned to the side, the board is locked at the side, but when the handle is turned down, the board is locked at the top, locking the companionway's sliding horizontal hatch. The handle is on both sides of the dropboard, so that locking may be done from the cabin or from the deck.

Do not assume that just because you sail only in semiprotected waters, you don't need a raised companionway sill on a

Fastnet storm slides ensure that the dropboard will remain locked in place. When the dropboard's handle is turned to the side (above), the board is locked at the side. When the handle is turned down (below), the board is locked at the top.

sinkable boat. A friend of mine reports witnessing a small cruiser sailing into a protected harbor just before being struck by a squall. Before sail could be lowered, the cruiser was knocked down by a strong puff. Her cockpit filled, downflooding her cabin, and she promptly sank. Her crew were all right after swimming a short distance to shore, and later they were able to raise the boat, but the accident never should have happened. It would not have occurred had there been a raised companionway sill or a lower dropboard locked in place.

Racing-cruisers or cruising-racers large enough to have decks that can be walked on need lifelines and pulpits. In fact, these safety features often are required by the rules under which the boats race, and details are available in the regulations. Be sure that lifelines are taut and above knee level to avoid tripping. Stanchions and pulpits must be through-bolted securely and hefty enough to take the weight of a heavy man being thrown against them. There should also be plenty of sturdy through-bolted handrails both above deck and below. Information on safety gear appears in chapter 4.

Boat Motion

Rough water can cause an amazing amount of motion. A boat can heave (lift or fall), sway (move sideways), yaw (turn on her vertical axis), pitch (rock on her transverse axis), roll (turn on her longitudinal axis), or surge (be pushed forward), and very often many of these movements will occur simultaneously. One must try to understand and visualize these motions, in order to adapt to them. Doing so will provide better balance and minimize staggering, prevent falls, and even help ease seasickness. On deck it is often easier to comprehend the motion by looking at the horizon and also the seas, studying their shapes and direction of movement. Are they lifting the boat, slamming against her bow, breaking under her stern, moving her bodily, rolling her from abeam? Once you under-

A high companionway sill and centerline hatch, as shown on this 23-foot Sea Sprite, are valuable safety features for windy weather sailing. (Barbara Hatch photo)

stand the effect of the seas and see how the boat is reacting, you can better adjust your body to the motion. Below decks it is more difficult to do this because you cannot see the water, but try to visualize what is happening. With a bit of practice, you are bound to improve.

Although some of the sensations experienced in a rough sea may be difficult to explain, it helps to understand how the boat and your body react to all the forces involved. First of all, an understanding of wave action may be beneficial. A wave is a kind of optical illusion in that the water within the wave does not move any great distance. This illusion has been compared with a mouse running under a rug. The humped part of the rug seems to move forward, but in fact the rug only moves up and down. The motion of the water molecules in a wave is essentially circular, as shown in the accompanying illustration. Each surface molecule has its own orbit, and its only movement is within a limited circle. Notice that a molecule in the trough between seas moves in the opposite direction from the wave motion; thus, a boat in that location will feel a slightly backward force against her hull. On the crest, the boat will sway or surge as she is pushed in the direction of the wave.

Another factor is the difference in wind strength between a wave's crest and its trough. The sails are at least partially blanketed in the trough, but they feel the wind's full force on the crest. Of course, the degree of blanketing depends on the size of the waves. Normally, a boat will be heeled and steadied

Motion of water molecules in a wave.

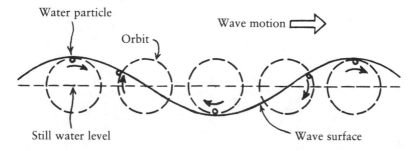

by her sails at the crest but may roll to weather in the trough. Boats with short rigs in very steep waves may even feel a back eddy from the wind in the trough.

An interesting phenomenon not commonly known is the effect of gravity on a wave slope. Unlike gravity on a ground slope, the downward force on a wave slope, which might be called wave slope gravity, is *perpendicular* to the water's surface. As a result, the boat and crew between trough and crest will be pulled down at an angle to the vertical rather than directly downward. The human body often will have the sensation of being level, and an inclinometer on the boat will even register level when it really is not. This is one reason why sailors tend to exaggerate the size of waves at sea, because they may be judging the height of a wave when they think they are level. In any case, it is comforting to know that the seas may not be as high as they appear to be, and it can be easier to cope with some of the motions when you can understand what your body is experiencing.

Rolling forces and wave slope gravity.

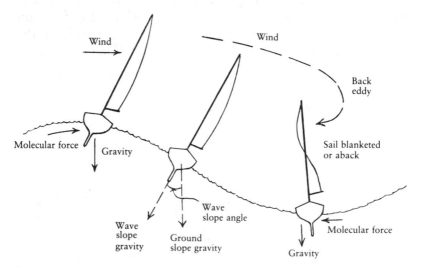

A boat's harshest treatment usually occurs when she is struck by breaking seas. These are waves so steep that they become unstable and topple forward, displacing their surface molecules from their orbits. There are two basic types of breakers—spillers and plungers. The former are most common at sea in deep water, and they break only at their very tops; plungers occur most often in shallow water, where they topple forward, with their tops crashing downward with considerable force. Whenever possible, avoid large plungers by steering around them. The power of any breaker can be minimized by slowing down or retreating from it. Try to avoid taking a plunger on the beam. (More about this appears in chapter 6.)

There are several ways to minimize a boat's motion in heavy seas. First of all, changing the boat's attitude with respect to the waves can help dramatically. This is especially true when the seas are on the beam and the boat is rolling vigorously. Sometimes the wave's period (the time it takes to pass a given point) is similar to the boat's rolling period, producing what is called synchronism, and in this case the rolling can be violent indeed. Changing the boat's heading so that the seas strike her abaft or forward of the beam can go far in alleviating this motion. Likewise, a boat that is pitching in head seas can obtain relief if she is headed off so that the waves strike her broader on the bow. It is also true that following seas can be more comfortable and cause fewer steering problems when they are taken at an angle between dead aft and the quarter. Some experimenting usually is necessary to tell just how the boat will react.

Plungers and spillers.

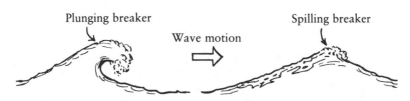

A tall rig can be a steadying factor in rough seas, as the weight aloft increases the vessel's roll inertia. There have even been a few cases when ocean sailors have hoisted weights aloft to alleviate an annoying roll. Of course, sails can have a strong damping effect on rolling when they are trimmed fairly flat. The greatest potential for damping occurs when the wind is abeam, but actual decrease in rolling will be greatest when the yacht is beating, because the sails are close-hauled and the boat is angled better to the approaching waves. The damping effect is minimal when the wind is astern, particularly when it is dead aft. On a centerboard boat, rolling often can be reduced by lowering the board to full depth.

The placement of weights in a boat also has a decided effect on her motion, particularly on pitching inertia. Most designers and racing sailors try to concentrate the major weights amidships to minimize hobbyhorsing, which has a devastating effect on boatspeed in head seas. This means that the engine, tanks, crew, and heavy gear should be as close as possible to the boat's transverse turning axis. (There are certain times, however, when weight should be spread apart; for example, the crew sometimes is stationed on each side of the boat to inhibit rolling in a following sea.) It might seem that a decrease in moment of inertia would cause greater motion, but excess weight in the boat's ends may increase her pitching period to the point where it more nearly corresponds to frequently encountered wave periods. Also, she will bury her bow more deeply in a sea and perhaps come to a near stop. A light-ended boat responds quickly to the waves and tends to ride over them more smoothly.

3

Rigs and Sails for Windy Weather

An obvious requirement for sailing in strong winds is a suitable rig with proper sails and a handy means of reducing them. High winds and rough seas over a prolonged period of time can impose considerable stress on the rig, so be sure to check that the various rigging components are installed and tuned according to safe, accepted practices. The larger the boat and the farther offshore she goes, the more important it is to rig her conservatively and with substantial margins of safety.

_____ Sail-Reduction Strategies

The heavy-air sail plan depends on the particular rig of the boat. Most modern boats are rigged as sloops, cutters, yawls, ketches, schooners, or cats. The last-mentioned rig may have one mast—in which case it is simply called a catboat—or it may have two masts and be either a cat ketch or cat schooner (having the taller mast aft). Cats have one primary characteristic: the forward mast is about as far forward as possible, and normally there is no headsail. The latest cat-rigged boats often have freestanding masts with no stays or shrouds. Although sloops and cutters have only one mast, the sloop has two basic working sails, while the cutter has three. The average modern cutter carries two working headsails, a forestaysail and a jib.

49

The yawl and ketch are similar in that each has two masts, with the shorter one being aft, but the yawl's mizzen is much smaller, and it usually is farther aft and acts as a balancing sail. The schooner yacht, with the larger of its two masts aft, is rarely seen today, but modern versions of this rig have a relatively tall foremast that can carry large jibs and spinnakers in light airs.

When it comes to sail reduction, multisailed and multimasted rigs have some advantage in that their sail plans are more versatile, allowing the complete removal of some sails without disturbing balance. Rigs with one or two sails usually (but not always) must be reefed to reduce sail. However, modern reefing systems are becoming increasingly easy to manage, and sail removal alone, without reefing, seldom is the optimal plan for prolonged sailing. Thus, the versatility of multimasted rigs is only really evident with a big boat, where the size and weight of sails makes them extremely difficult to handle.

The main objective when reducing sail is the preservation of helm balance. For most boats, the perfectly balanced helm is a slight weather helm in a moderate breeze. When this is the case, the helm usually is slack or neutral in light airs, but the tendency to automatically luff up increases gradually as the boat heels more and more in a freshening breeze. Some weather helm is desirable, particularly in small centerboarders, as a safeguard in helping to prevent capsizing. Also, it can augment keel lift and help the helmsman work the boat to windward in rough seas. But too much weather helm is literally a drag, as the rudder held over too far causes great resistance, which slows the boat and tires the helmsman. Furthermore, freestanding spade-type rudders are particularly subject to stalling, thereby destroying the rudder's effectiveness. Lee helm should almost never be tolerated, particularly in a fresh breeze. Should the boat develop a lee helm, set more sail aft, or reduce sail forward.

With any well-designed boat, good balance comes from optimizing the relationship of the geometric center of the sails, commonly called the total center of effort (TCE), to the center of lateral resistance (CLR), the geometric center of the under-

Sloop   Yawl   Ketch

Cutter   Schooner

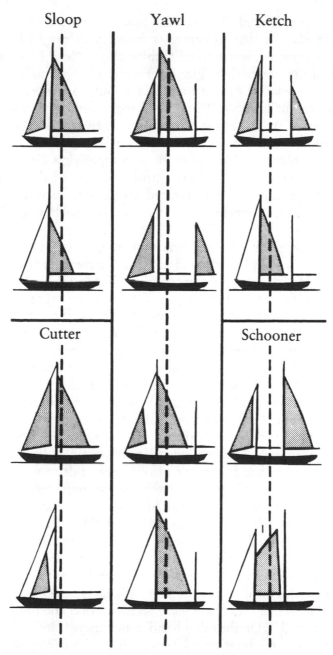

Preserving helm balance under reduced sail.

water part of the hull. The modern boat is balanced by shaping the sail plan so that its center is forward of the CLR. This distance forward, which naval architects call "lead," varies for different rigs and hull designs, but for the average modern keel sloop of moderate proportions it is about 15 percent of the load waterline length (LWL). In sail reduction the lead should be preserved or perhaps moved slightly forward to counteract any extra weather helm caused by heeling. Some basic sail reduction plans are shown in the accompanying illustration, which shows the TCEs (heavy broken lines) of the various boats under full sail. Each reduced sail plan is fairly well balanced, having a similar amount of sail on each side of the broken line.

Of course, there are combinations other than those shown, and reduced sail plans depend to a large extent on sea conditions and the particular point of sailing. For instance, if you are running off or broad reaching, you might want more sail area forward to counteract any tendency for the boat to broach-to; i.e., round up inadvertently, coming beam to the sea. However, on a beat or close reach in rough water, you might need some sail aft to keep your bow from being knocked downwind by the seas. When the waves are steep and breaking, keep each reduced sail reasonably high off the deck to avoid blanketing and to keep its foot away from solid water or heavy spray.

An important general principle of sail reduction is to keep the reduced sails as close together as possible. Particularly when sailing upwind, the sails afford greater drive with small area when they can work together aerodynamically. If two properly trimmed sails are close together on a point of sailing that minimizes blanketing and backwinding, they can help each other through circulation or slot effects and/or diversion of the airflow. Partly for this reason, a forestaysail set close to a reduced mainsail in a hard blow is often better than a small jib set far forward. Also, the forestaysail is easier to handle when it is farther aft, where there is less motion and more deck space around it. On the other hand, when there is less wind but a steep chop, the boat may very well need a fairly large jib to power through the seas.

With a yawl or ketch, it often is convenient to drop the mainsail when caught in a sudden squall, but the more effective combination for prolonged sailing in a blow is one that concentrates the driving sails somewhat forward of amidships and uses the mizzen merely for balance. How well I remember being trounced by our competition during a stormy race when the yawl on which I was crew carried only a sizable jib and mizzen. When we changed to a slightly smaller jib and set the reefed main, the boat came to life and outsailed her rivals.

Finally—despite a healthy human tendency to err on the side of caution—sails should not be reduced too much, particularly in choppy waters. You need a sail plan that will stop excessive heeling but one that will provide enough power to drive the boat through the seas.

—————————— Basic Reefing Systems

There are a number of different ways to reduce the size of a sail, but most modern methods are based on one of two general reefing systems: (1) rolling one edge of the sail, similar to the operation of a roller window shade, or (2) tying down a portion of the sail with reef points and earings (reefing lines). Roller methods have the advantage of infinite variability, but optimal shape usually is sacrificed. The old, but still used, method of rolling the sail's foot around a rotating boom most often produces a shape that is too full when deeply reefed; there is no completely satisfactory way to stretch the foot tight with an outhaul. Luff roller reefing, used most often with a jib, also produces an overly full sail with its deepest draft (curvature) generally too far aft; the luff cannot be tensioned. A further problem with luff rolling is tortional twisting of the stay on which the jib is set, but this can be minimized by using one of the systems with a grooved aluminum foil rather than a wire to support the luff. A problem with boom rotation is that when the reef is deep, the outboard end of the boom droops, creating a tripping hazard and greater encouragement for the clew to creep forward. Most of these problems can be alleviated, however, and partial solutions are discussed in chapter 5.

The most satisfactory form of reefing for boomed sails is the so-called jiffy (or slab) system. This is similar to old-fashioned reef-points reefing, except that it is not as complicated and there is less dependence on the points (short lines in the middle of the sail) for support and shaping. The primary load-carrying line is a clew earing, which is led from the outboard

A Cal 28 roller reefed. Notice the prominent fold in the main-sail just forward of the battens—a result of not being able to apply outhaul tension. (Courtesy Joe Fuller)

end of the boom up through a reef grommet in the sail's leech, then back down to a cheek block on the boom (or to an internal sheave), and then forward to a winch. The reef grommet at the tack usually is attached to a hook at the gooseneck. A lacing line or a few reef points are needed at the boom's middle to hold up the bunt (loose part of the sail that hangs down). The usual procedure is to set up the boom's topping lift, ease the sheet, slack the halyard until the luff cringle (reef grommet) reaches the tack hook, rehoist after the grommet is hooked, then winch the leech cringle down close to the boom. Sometimes a tack earing is used to haul down the luff cringle. When the halyard and both earings are led back to the cockpit, the basic operation can be performed without going forward. The great advantage of this method, aside from handiness, is that it can produce a properly shaped reduced sail.

When installing the clew earing, be sure its eye strap and cheek block are sufficiently far aft to tension the sail's foot properly. The earing should pull down and aft at an angle that approximately bisects the clew. One way to ensure that the angle is about right is to tie the dead end of the earing a little farther aft than directly under the reef cringle, pass the line up through the grommet and then down to a block at the very end of the boom (see accompanying illustration). You can tie the earing's end around the boom through a foot grommet as shown, or tie it to an eye strap on the boom under the reef cringle, or tie it to the cringle to form an extra purchase. Another alternative is to mount the cheek block on a slide so that its location is adjustable. An advantage of this arrangement is that the foot tension can be fine-adjusted for various conditions. For instance, sometimes a bit more slack is helpful for power in rough seas.

When it comes to reducing the area of boomless headsails, the most satisfactory plan for prolonged upwind sailing is a change of jibs. A smaller jib specifically designed for heavier weather conditions almost always will be better in terms of construction, shape, and weight than a reefed light-weather sail. If there is an inner forestaysail, however, it is very convenient to have an outer roller-furling jib that can be reduced

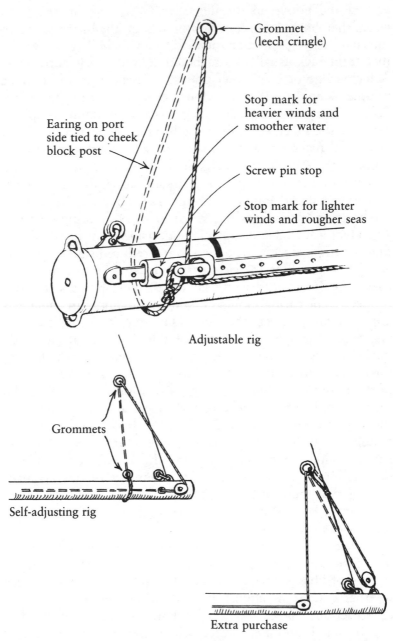

The clew ends of three jiffy reefing systems.

gradually in a freshening wind until it is completely furled. Then, when it is really blowing, the flatter and perhaps heavier forestaysail, which is the right distance from the main, can take over the duties of the jib.

Details at the tack end of a jiffy-reefed mainsail. Cringle rings and hooks at the gooseneck simplify the operation.

On a seagoing boat or any shorthanded cruiser that relies on jib changes for sail reduction, it is important that the head-sail be attached to the stay with hanks rather than held to a slotted foil by a boltrope in a groove; hanks (or snaphooks) allow the luff to remain attached to the stay at all times when lowering and hoisting. For roller jibs that are not changed often, hanks are not vital, and in fact a slotted foil is more efficient in such a situation. For extensive offshore cruising, however, look into one of the systems that uses sail slides in the luff groove, such as Famet Marine's Reefurl or Supermarine's Superfurl.

Points reefing for headsails is controversial. It is not as trouble-free as it appears to be, because it requires that a lot of points be tied in very tightly to keep the reefed portion of the headsail from filling with water or coming untied when it flaps violently. Also, lightweight and even medium-weight jibs can be stretched out of shape by frequent exposure to heavy winds in the reefed configuration. Heavy reinforcing patches will help, but this may harm the sail's light-weather efficiency when it is unreefed. Do not consider reef points in a headsail unless it is a fairly small, heavy sail intended for fresh winds.

Heavy-Air Sails

Virtually all modern sailcloth is synthetic, and it is available in a firm or a relatively soft finish. A sail made of firm cloth tends to hold its shape better in a fresh breeze, but it is stiff, slippery, awkward to handle, and difficult to stow. Racing boats need such sails for the greatest possible speed, but for a nonracer, particularly a shorthanded cruiser, choose softer cloth. A good choice for working sails is tightly woven, heat-set, uncoated Dacron (polyester).

Working sails that are seldom changed—such as mainsails, mizzens, and forestaysails—should be made of reasonably heavy material so that they can stand up to almost any kind of weather. According to an old rule-of-thumb, you determine ideal mainsail weight in ounces per yard by adding the boat's length overall (LOA) to the sail's luff length and dividing by 10. (Some modern sails, with superior weave and construction, might be slightly lighter). Despite their smaller size, mizzens and forestaysails should not be much, if any, lighter than mainsails, because they might be needed in very heavy winds. A roller jib should be considerably heavier than a light No. 1 (largest) genoa jib if it will be carried partially rolled. A daysailer or overnighter used only in protected waters need not have sails quite as heavy as those of an offshore cruiser, but it is wise to keep in mind that any boat anywhere can be caught by an unexpected blow.

Sail stability or resistance to stretch is obtained not only from the finish and weight of the cloth but also from the sail's cut. Partly as a result of competition among sailmakers, there is a great variety in sail cuts nowadays, particularly on sophisticated racing yachts. Most panel arrangements, however, are variations and/or combinations of several basic cuts: (1) vertical cut, with the seams running parallel to the leech; (2) crosscut, with the seams running at right angles to the leech; (3) miter cut, having a miter seam more or less bisecting the clew with seams above the miter at right angles to the leech and seams below the miter at right angles to the foot; and (4) radial cut, with the seams radiating toward the sail's center from each corner.

These cuts primarily minimize bias stretch (actually elongation), which results when the load direction is diagonal to the thread line. The sailmaker tries to orient the cloth panels so that in the areas of greatest stress, the weave is square with the load direction.

The leech is the side of a sail most heavily loaded when close trimmed in a fresh breeze, so this highly stressed area traditionally has been vertical or crosscut. A modern—but more complicated and more expensive—alternative is the bi-radial cut, with the seams radiating from the head and clew (see accompanying illustration). Of the sail's three corners, the head and especially the clew are most heavily loaded, so the biradial sail is very effective in reducing corner stretch. Another way to deal with corner loading is to use radial patches, as shown in the illustration. When conventional corner patches are used on a heavy-weather sail, you will feel more comfortable if there are webbing reinforcements radiating inward from the corner grommet. Whatever the method of construction, be sure that the clew and head are very heavily reinforced.

A heavy-air sail generally should be cut flatter than one intended for light weather, and its maximum camber (depth of curvature) should be slightly farther forward than normal. This counteracts the usual tendency of the draft or camber to move aft in a fresh wind. When a sail is too full in its after part, its thrust is converted more to drag and heeling forces—just what you don't need when you are trying to reduce heel and gain power to drive through rough seas. A relatively simple

Sail cuts.

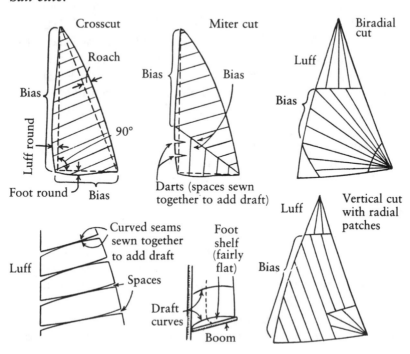

way to reduce draft is to limit or decrease the luff round (or convex curvature at the luff), as shown in the illustration. One way to pull the draft forward is to tension the luff, and this method works well when the cloth panels are angled at the luff to allow some bias stretch. Notice that all of the basic sail cuts previously described allow some bias stretch at the luff, but the crosscut sail allows the most. The softer sails respond most satisfactorily to change of shape through variations in luff tension. (More about this appears in chapter 5.)

When ordering a sail intended for use in strong winds, be sure that it is triple-stitched. Although some sailmakers disagree, it has been said that dark polyester thread is more resistant to sun rot than white thread, and I have found this to be true. Special coatings such as Tuffseam are useful in protecting seams in vulnerable areas from chafe. Keep firmly in mind that when an old sail blows out in heavy winds, it usually is the stitching that fails. If the thread is broken, worn, or suspect in any area, take the sail to your sailmaker and have it extensively restitched.

Headsails intended for fresh winds should have minimal overlap, and their leeches should be fairly hollow (with a reverse roach or concave curvation). A sturdy leech line prevents the rapid leech flutter that often occurs when the sail is trimmed flat in a breeze. This flutter, often called "motorboating," not only is annoying but also can be damaging to the sail. The sail's foot should be cut high, with the clew far above the rail so that seas will not break against the bottom of the sail. There should be minimal round or convex curvature at the foot.

Battens are vulnerable in windy weather. They should be made of plastic or fiberglass, as wood battens can break when they slam against the rigging in a blow. Offset batten pockets are fine, but there should also be eyelets and lashing lines for the worst conditions. I have seen battens thrown from their offset pockets when the sail shakes violently. A batten should press firmly against the aft edge of its pocket. Usually this is achieved with elastic material in the bottom of the pocket, but elastic soon grows tired. Nowadays, the best solution is to have the batten as long as its pocket and use soft plastic protectors on the batten's ends to guard against chafe.

The heavy-air sails needed will vary, of course, with the size and intended use of the boat. Just about any boat, however, should have a small, No. 2 working jib that will balance well with a deeply reefed mainsail. This jib should have a fairly long luff and a moderately high clew that is well forward of the mast. Despite the fact that a long luff raises the sail's center of effort, the forward part of the sail furnishes most of its drive, and substantial area is needed up front to power through rough seas. The actual size of this sail depends on such factors as the size of the foretriangle, the stability of the boat, and the likelihood that a storm jib will be carried. Discuss these matters with a sailmaker.

Every offshore boat should carry a spitfire (a small storm headsail) and a storm trysail. Some boats even carry a Swedish main (a small mainsail with hollow leech and no headboard or battens). This sail is well shaped for a blow and avoids potential problems from battens, but it is more troublesome to set it than to reef the working main. The Swedish main is not necessary for the average boat, especially one with a modern jiffy or slab reefing system that can do its job effectively.

On the other hand, a storm trysail might well be needed as a substitute for the mainsail in Force 7 or 8 conditions and above. It has an area of about the same size or smaller than a deep-reefed main but is battenless. It has the advantage over a Swedish main of being loose footed and cut with a low clew, so it can be sheeted to the deck and need not be attached to the boom. It is seldom desirable to have a boom thrashing about, but when you need to do a lot of tacking, you can hoist the trysail a bit higher than normal to allow use of the main boom and its sheet. This avoids the need to change sheets when changing tacks.

The trysail, made of fairly soft cloth about the same weight as the main, is cut very flat to minimize luffing and heeling. Its tack should be high not only to facilitate deck sheeting but also to keep the sail clear of the furled mainsail. To figure the recommended size, square the mainsail luff dimension and multiply the result by .05, which gives the trysail area in square feet. The head of the sail should go close to a point on the mast where there is a stay or shroud pulling forward to oppose the trysail's pull aft.

A combination of storm trysail and No. 2 working jib allows some progress to windward in Force 8 conditions. (R.C. Henderson photo)

Probably the best arrangement for attaching the luff to the mast is a special trysail track that accepts sail slides. The sail can be carried bent on but bagged. Then, when it is needed, the main is lowered and the trysail can be hoisted immediately on

Kelpie's spitfire, a versatile sail that can be carried either as a storm jib on the foremost stay or a storm staysail set on an inner stay. (R.C. Henderson photo)

its own track after the halyard is switched over. If the trysail is carried on the mainsail track, there should be a gate in the track a couple of feet from its bottom so that the bent-on trysail slides can be stacked below the gate. When it is necessary to change sails, the mainsail's slides can be removed through the gate as the sail is lowered, and the trysail is ready to be hoisted. The only disadvantage of this method is that when it comes time to rehoist the main, its slides will have to be bent on, but this seldom is a serious problem after the blow has moderated.

The spitfire is a versatile sail that can be carried either as a storm jib set on the foremost stay or a storm staysail set on an inner stay. On my 37-footer, which has no permanent forestaysail, I carry a removable stay that I shackle to a mast eye at the hounds (the spot where the lower shrouds attach just under the spreaders) before *Kelpie* goes offshore, and I lash the stay's lower end to a forward lower shroud. Then, in the event of a strong blow, I bring the stay's lower end forward to a strong deck eye and secure it there with a pelican hook (a lever-type hook held closed with a slip ring). When needed, this arrangement adds a forestay on which to hank a storm staysail, for the advantages mentioned earlier. The sail, shown in the accompanying photograph, might seem too small to many sailors, but the recommended size for a spitfire is .025 times the height of the foretriangle squared.

Masting and Rigging

The rigging of a sailboat is an involved subject that cannot be presented in great depth here. The subject is covered much more thoroughly in my book *Understanding Rigs and Rigging*, published by International Marine Publishing Company in 1985.

The standing rigging, consisting of stays and shrouds, must be installed and tensioned in such a manner that the mast does not invert or bend the wrong way, and it must be held reasonably steady in a seaway. This means that the mast should not be allowed to wave (move at the top) or pump (move excessively in the middle) when pounding into rough seas. Although some small racing boats carry rather floppy rigs with fairly slack rigging, most boats of any size should carry their rigging fairly taut, or ar least snug enough to steady the mast.

Another consideration is panel length, the distance on the mast between points where the rigging attaches. In general, the shorter the panel the stiffer the mast for a given mast sectional size.

A mast can be kept straight if the rigging is attached in an opposing system that prevents bending moments. Such a system requires that the components be directly opposite, with one wire being attached on one side of the mast at almost the same altitude as an opposing wire on the other side. Some masts are designed to bend aft in order to help flatten sails in a breeze, but a mast never should be allowed to bend forward in a fresh headwind, and it should not bend sideways more than a very slight amount. Be sure there is sufficient adjustable secondary rigging, such as running backstays, that can be set up easily to control bending and prevent pumping. Also, make sure that shroud angles (between the mast and the shrouds) are greater than about 10 degrees to minimize compression loading, which contributes to undesirable mast bend. For further information on shroud loads and formulas for determining mast and rigging strength, see Appendix.

Safety Considerations

A most important concern with rigging is minimizing metal fatigue. For the most part, this requires proper rigging alignment and the use of toggles—U-shaped fittings with pins that act as universal joints allowing rotation in both fore-and-aft and lateral directions (see illustration). Universal joints are important to prevent bending of the wire and all connecting metal parts, such as tangs (mast connection straps or hooks), swaged fittings (compression sleeves squeezed on the wire ends), and chainplates (straps or eyes connecting the rigging to the boat). These parts must be properly aligned, following a straight line through their shroud or stay from the deck to the mast. When the line is not straight, the metal can bend back and forth when the rig loading varies, as it normally does in rough-weather conditions. Everyone knows how easily a metal coat hanger will snap after it has been bent back and forth a number of times. Work-hardening and fatigue can also occur in a sailboat's rig, although rigging wire and fittings are infinitely more resistant to failure. As long as there are universal joints at the lower ends of all shrouds and stays and at the upper end of any stay that carries a large sail, and all rigging is in alignment, there should be little to worry about.

Successful sailing in dusty weather also requires sound running rigging and related hardware. See that all your fittings are strong. I am wary of cast aluminum fittings, because I have seen too many of them break. Fittings of forged bronze or stainless steel are far more reliable. Turning blocks that turn a sheet 180 degrees must be especially strong, because the load on the block is doubled. If the load on the line leading to the block is 500 pounds, for example, the load on the line leading away from the block is 500 pounds, and this produces a total strain of 1,000 pounds on the block. When the line is turned less than 180 degrees, the strain will be less than double. A

Toggles allow rotation both fore-and-aft and laterally, reducing metal fatigue in rigging.

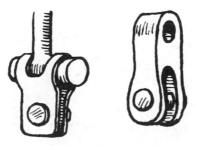

rough method of estimating loads on the block is shown in the accompanying illustration. Strain on a sheet can be calculated with the formula .00431 x A x V^2 = load in pounds, where A is the sail area and V is the wind velocity. The breaking strengths or safe working loads for fittings usually are listed in hardware catalogs. Safe working loads normally are considered 40 percent or less of the breaking strength. Remember that the failure of fittings can cause serious injuries, so be sure that the line will break before the fitting does.

Beware of fittings that open up when a sail is flogging. It is best to tie sheets to their sails, providing greater security and reducing the danger of personal injury from a loose metal

A rough method of estimating load on a sheet block.

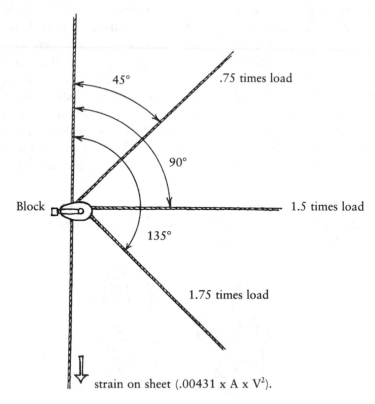

45°   .75 times load

90°

Block   1.5 times load

135°

1.75 times load

strain on sheet (.00431 x A x V^2).

fitting. Bear in mind, though, that knots can weaken lines, so sheets that are tied on should be extra heavy. Some snatch-blocks and snapshackles also can open up, so lash or tape the fittings closed when you are using them in a real blow. It is best that lead blocks for storm sails be nonopening, solid types. Be sure that all deck fittings are through-bolted and that they have large washers or backing plates.

Have winches that are large enough to allow proper trimming of the sails in a breeze. It is all too common to see boats struggling along on a windy day with their sails ashake and excessively slack luffs causing disastrous shaping. This often occurs because there is insufficient winch power for properly tensioning sheets and halyards or downhauls. Mast winches in particular need lock-on handles that will not fall off when the boat heels. Also, see that all tackles have sufficient purchase for easy handling in windy weather. Sheets and other lines, regardless of their strength, should be of sufficient diameter to allow easy gripping. If you have a bail on your mast to which halyards are secured when not in use, see that it is well secured. One time a friend of mine was prevented from hoisting any sails during a blow because the screws securing the bail sheared off and the halyards streamed off to leeward, well out of reach.

Other parts of the rig with a potential for problems are spreaders and booms. Be sure that the spreaders are thoroughly inspected at least once a season. They must be firmly secured to the shrouds, and the angle between shroud and spreader should be the same above and below the spreader. Remember that a broken or slipped spreader could lead to a broken mast. Spreader sockets need special attention. I prefer stainless steel sockets to those of cast aluminum, as the latter can have hidden flaws. If you have cast sockets, examine them carefully for cracks. Also, be sure that spreaders are pinned into their sockets so that they cannot slip out as the shrouds go slack on the leeward side when the boat is heeled.

A boom is particularly subject to bending stress if its sheet is secured to its middle. When this is the case, see that blocks for the sheet's tackle are spread apart along the boom so that the downward load is distributed more or less evenly over a wide area. Concentrating the load in one spot could break the boom when it is bowsed down in a strong wind. Be sure the booms do not droop so low at their outboard ends that they could trip when the boat rolls. Also, check that the boom is not so long that it could strike the backstay during a jibe when the boom rides upward. I have had this happen on two occasions. Additional information on rig checks and underway inspections in general appears in chapter 5.

4

To Sail or Not to Sail

How often the novice sailor, even the veteran, has stood dockside on a windy day contemplating whether or not to go sailing. The decision is often very difficult, because it depends on appraisals based on a number of variables. Among the considerations should be: the degree of his experience, familiarity with his boat, her seaworthiness, equipment, crew capability, general weather trend, local conditions, wave characteristics, and availability of rescue facilities.

Experience, in this case, has to do with the number of times you have sailed in windy conditions. You should know what to expect in regard to seasickness, discomfort, seamanship requirements, and boat behavior in general. Weigh carefully your local knowledge and familiarity with the waters on which you will be sailing. You need to know from what directions squalls usually come, whether the strongest gusts are channeled down a river, or whether a certain shore affords good protection. Experience can offer such knowledge as where the waters are most choppy or relatively smooth and how the current flowing past a point affects the seas.

Familiarity with your boat and the way she handles in windy weather is certainly a major consideration. You need to have some idea of whether she is stiff or tender, how wet she is, whether she tends to pound or develop a strong weather helm, how she tacks in head seas. You also need to be aware of her downwind directional stability (yawing characteristics), the

71

capabilities for trimming and flattening sails, reefing systems, and the nature of the rig in regard to keeping the mast steady.

Even if it is just a windy day and no storm is expected, you must know the degree of protection afforded by your harbor in order to assess the condition of exposed waters offshore. It is particularly helpful when there is some nearby location from which you can catch a glimpse of the open water to see what conditions are like outside. Then you can study the waves with binoculars and observe the behavior and sail reductions of other boats. Bear in mind that when you look in the direction the wind is blowing (as opposed to looking against the wind), the seas will appear more smooth and whitecaps will not be so noticeable. Also, a wind blowing off the shore on which you are located will not greatly disturb the waters near that shore. Remember that when you sail from behind the shelter of high banks, buildings, or tall trees, you will be passing from a relatively calm area to an exposed one and suddenly will receive the full force of the wind. Be aware of gaps in the shoreline through which the wind can funnel. Never even consider going out on a windy day without adequate equipment. Be sure your boat has all the heavy-weather sails you might need. If she has an engine, know its condition and make sure there is sufficient fuel. Has she enough Coast Guard-approved PFDs (personal flotation devices)—one for each member of the crew? Is there a satisfactory means of bailing? How about ground tackle? (You might want to anchor in a sudden squall.) Be sure there is at least one safety harness for working on the foredeck, and don't forget your foul-weather gear. Even on a bright, sunny day, there may be plenty of spray blowing aft when you are driving to windward.

In order to make a thoughtful decision about whether or not to venture out, it helps to be able to visualize what the sailing may be like. Let's picture two typical boats that the average nonracing sailor might consider taking out in semiprotected waters on a windy day. The first is an open-cockpit, centerboard daysailer about 17 feet long. She has considerable initial stability and stands up quite well to her sail in a breeze, but obviously she can capsize if she is handled carelessly or overburdened with too much sail. The second example is the 35-foot cruising sloop used in chapter 1 to evaluate the effects from various Beaufort Scale wind forces. In order to help the novice and perhaps encourage the timid sailor, I will attempt here to describe how these boats might behave in Force 5 and 6 conditions. Of course, I can only generalize because of the differences between individual boats and the variety of conditions in various sailing waters.

In lower Force 5 winds, our particular daysailer will have about all the sail she wants with a small jib and full main, and she will need a fairly heavy crew on the rail. Going to windward, she has her rail down, and the mainsheet may need easing in the puffs. The crew will lean far out to windward when the rail dips low. The boat will be jumping off the waves and occasionally pounding like a bass drum, but she is strongly built, and this does no harm. Spray and occasionally a dollop of wave on the lee side slops into the cockpit, but this modern daysailer has ample flotation and transom bailers (holes through the transom covered with flaps that may be opened to let the water drain out).

As she bears away from the wind, the boat picks up speed and frequently screams onto a semiplane when the waves roll under the hull at a favorable angle. The hull seems to lift and accelerate, throwing out sheets of spray on either side of the bow, providing a most exciting ride. Since progress to windward is not the goal here, the centerboard should be raised about halfway. This will increase stability by shortening the heeling arm and reducing any tendency to trip on the board, while moving the center of lateral resistance farther aft to decrease weather helm.

The waves have breaking tops, but they are not high enough to cause any problems, because we are in moderately protected waters. When we sail off the wind, on a run or broad reach, the seas may occasionally slew about the stern just a bit, so we need to anticipate this motion and respond quickly with the tiller. Be sure the centerboard is far enough down to enhance steering control, and keep the jib trimmed in a bit

Boat	Force 5	Force 6	Force 7	Force 8	Force 8+
Day Sailer 17 foot centerboard					
Rhodes 19 fin keel					
West Wight Potter 19 drop keel					
J-24 short fin keel considerable mast bend					
Cape Dory 25 full keel masthead rig					

Sail-reduction strategies for representative production boats. These sail reductions are general and need not be relied on literally. Exact strategy would depend on such factors as the number of crewmembers, sea conditions, whether the boat is

Boat	Force 5	Force 6	Force 7	Force 8	Force 8+
Thunder Bird 26 foot fin keel small fore-triangle					
Cal 2–30 15/16 rig					
Cabot 36 cutter					
Ohlson 38 sloop with removable staysail stay					
Bermuda 40 keel/center-board yawl					

racing or cruising, and how the boat is rigged. The reef points illustrated are primarily symbolic, since stock boats are fitted with roller reefing, and many boats with jiffy reefing use a lacing line rather than reef points to gather the bunt of the sail.

flatter than normal to help hold off the bow. Keep the boom vang snug to remove excessive mainsail twist and hold the boom down.

At the upper end of Force 5, we are beginning to be over-burdened. It is difficult to keep the rail out when reaching, considerable water is coming aboard, and the helm is less manageable. The time has definitely come to reduce sail. We can always drop one sail if it is necessary to shorten down in a hurry, but better balance will result from reefing the mainsail. This will decrease power and heeling while moving the center of effort of the sail plan farther forward to help reduce excessive weather helm. Having a small, two-sail plan also will help us tack in sloppy seas, because we may be stopped by a wave when coming about, and the jib can be backed to pull us around onto the new tack. (More about this appears in chapter 6).

If it should suddenly breeze up to Force 6 or higher, we will need even more reduction in sail, and then it might make sense to drop one sail. If the mast is located fairly far forward and the main has been deeply reefed, balance should not be affected too badly by lowering the jib. On the other hand, when a boat with a small jib needs drastic reduction and the course for sheltered waters is downwind, you can drop the main. Some boats can even be sailed to windward under jib alone. Balance will suffer, but if the boat has a lot of beam aft, heeling often will alleviate or counteract lee helm. Under jib alone, the boat may be difficult if not impossible to tack, but you can change tacks by jibing around. Bear in mind, however, that once the main is down, it may be very difficult to get it back up again because the boat will no longer hold her bow into the wind. Before dropping the main, be sure that your safe course is comfortably downwind.

In the upper range of Force 6, the small centerboard day-sailer should stay in port or return home if caught out. An exception could exist if the boat were manned by highly experienced, skillful crew using small, flat sails specifically designed for heavy winds and when the sailing locale afforded reasonably warm, protected waters with nearby rescue facilities.

Our second boat, the 35-foot cruising sloop with ballasted keel, is more able than the daysailer and can cope better with strong winds. In lower Force 5 conditions, she will be driving steadily to windward with more consistent speed. A lot of spray will be flying, but she will have the power to punch through the

An Invicta sloop close reaching in Force 5 conditions. Notice that on this point of sailing, the low-cut genoa can scoop up seas. (Courtesy Mrs. Fred Thomas)

seas without being slowed very much, and her softer bilge (rounded bottom) will inhibit pounding. For maximum performance, she should be carrying a fairly small No. 2 genoa. This jib's moderate overlap and long luff length provides more power than a working jib, but the latter is preferable if comfort is the major objective. It will slow the boat, producing an easier motion with less wetness, and reduce heeling.

Bearing off from the beat and easing the sheets causes an increase in speed, but not to the same extent as with the day-sailer. The cruiser is a relatively heavy-displacement boat, and she creates a bigger wave system. With the sheets slacked, the jib's foot may be in a position to scoop up the bow wave as the boat plunges. If this happens, alter course to minimize scooping, and/or use a tack pendant to raise the foot above the seas, or change to a high-cut jib. On a beam reach, the boat is dipping her lee rail and she has a bit more weather helm than desirable, so it is time to ease the mainsheet until there is a prominent bulge in the sail abaft the mast. Luffing the main is perfectly acceptable, but allowing it to flap for a long time is not. Prolonged flapping in a strong wind can damage or at least shorten the life of a sail.

As the boat bears away onto a broad reach, she gains stability, and there is not as much problem of scooping up seas with the jib. She will yaw a bit more from the quartering seas, but the helmsman can counteract this easily. It helps to have a buoyant stern with generous freeboard aft so that following seas, reinforced by the boat's stern wave, will not slop over the after rail.

Before the wind reaches Force 6, the main will need reefing, and above Force 6, a smaller, heavy-air jib definitely will be needed. If it is a small genoa, its foot should be well raised with a generous tack pendant.

The seas will be getting fairly rough; so don oilskins, see that all loose gear is securely stowed below, and be sure that any vulnerable openings such as portholes are closed. You may want a safety line when working forward, and if the galley is in use, the cook should be wearing a safety belt. The stove is gimbaled to swing 35 degrees on either tack, so pots can stay on top until the boat's rail begins to bury. In these conditions in moderately protected waters, the crew can carry on almost as usual, but it is wise to move a little more deliberately and always hang on tight. When the weather is agreeable, the experience is one of pure exhilaration.

One final word of advice concerning your decision about whether or not to go sailing in windy weather: Select your crew with care. If you have a sizable boat, be sure you have enough people to winch, reef, dock, and perform any other procedure that will be more difficult in a blow. Even a small boat may need sufficient crew weight to hold her down in puffs and prevent excessive heeling. Of course, it's perfectly possible to sail shorthanded when the boat is properly rigged, but be sure your crew has reasonable skill and experience.

————— If You Are Caught in a Blow

Let's suppose now that you are out sailing and it gradually breezes up, with a hard blow seeming likely. Perhaps a squall is threatening. At this point, you will need to make a number of onboard preparations.

• If you or your crew are susceptible to seasickness, take seasickness pills (or other remedial action). The most popular drugs, such as Dramamine, Marezine, and Bonine, in fact, should be taken far ahead of time. Even Transderm, the stick-on disk that delivers a gradual dose of scopolamine, may take two or three hours to work. If you have waited too long before taking the more popular pills, you might try Bucladin S, a small, yellowish pill that you hold under your tongue. It is absorbed into the body without any need to swallow. (With this remedy, there is no danger of losing a pill in the stomach from vomiting.) Bucladin S requires a doctor's prescription, but it seems to be highly effective and is less apt to cause drowsiness.
• Next, don foul-weather gear. Once you get wet, particularly in the salty ocean, it takes almost forever to dry off. Also,

The Valiant 40 Mooneshine *being singlehanded by Francis Stokes. She is well balanced under reefed main and forestaysail. (Brian Harrison photo)*

see that your clothing and bedding is all stowed in water-proof lockers or bags. If you will be sailing in very cold weather, carry a dry suit, which is so waterproof that you can swim in it. It also guards against hypothermia. Sailing gloves (with open fingers) are also a good idea, as they not only keep hands warm but also guard against rope burns.

• Prior to a storm, carefully check your navigation. Take bearings to note exactly where you are, because visibility later might be drastically impaired.

• Before the seas become extremely rough and the spray starts flying, raise your companionway dodger if you have one. This affords protection not only to the forward end of the cockpit but also to the quarter berths and the chart table below (when it is near the companionway). On *Kelpie,* we also have a small curtain that pulls across the quarter berth/chart-table seat for added protection. A dodger that covers the entire width of the cockpit is particularly valuable in wet weather, but it must have plenty of clear plastic windows for the best possible visibility. There should be a dodger coaming (preferably unperforated by holes for halyard leads) at the forward end of the dodger to keep out water. On offshore boats where visibility is not so critical, you can also increase comfort with weather cloths rigged between the lifelines and the toerail surrounding and just forward of the cockpit area.

• Unless you are racing, make all sail changes and reef down early, because these tasks are infinitely more difficult after the seas have become rough.

• Close all ports or windows and dog all hatches that are not being used. Cover all vulnerable ventilators, but correctly installed Dorades should remain uncovered to admit air below.

• Close seacocks on all unneeded through-hull fittings. Be sure to shut off the drains on off-center sinks to prevent flooding when the boat is well heeled.

• Pump the bilge as dry as you can so that water cannot roll up underneath the bunks and into low lockers.

• See that all loose gear on deck is stowed properly or lashed securely.

- Check that all gear below decks is well stowed and, in particular, see that any heavy object is well secured.
- Be sure that water cannot flood the engine through the exhaust port. If you have any doubt, run the engine during the roughest weather. Some boats have exhaust shutoff valves, but be sure to open these before starting the engine.
- Have your ground tackle well secured but ready for use in case you need to anchor.
- Don a PFD or flotation jacket, and perhaps a safety harness, if the seas become extremely rough.
- If you are towing a dinghy, try to get it on board before the weather deteriorates. If this is impossible, remove the oars and oarlocks (this should in fact have been done before you departed), and pay out the painter to full scope. When running off, dinghies towed close astern have been thrown against their mother vessels' sterns, so they should be towed far astern. Once when I was caught in a storm towing a dinghy, she behaved like a hooked fish, diving and tumbling. Fortunately, I had her at the end of a long nylon painter attached to a well-bolted bow eye, and she came through the experience unscathed. If in doubt about the strength of the bow eye, tie the end of the painter around a strong thwart as well.
- Communicate with your crew. When a storm is brewing, tell them your plan of action and what you expect them to do. If you go forward to handle sails, assign an experienced person to the helm.
- Prepare a Thermos of hot coffee, tea, or bouillon before a storm commences. This is comforting and boosts morale.
- Keep a lookout at all times, particularly in crowded waters. In a storm, boats may be moving in unexpected directions.
- Before and during the blow, stay calm. This helps you think more clearly and makes the crew more confident. Sudden air mass thunderstorms seldom last long, and you can usually wait them out. As long as you have a good boat and she is well equipped, you should be all right. Remember that forethought and seamanship can overcome just about any challenge you should happen to meet.

5

Sailhandling in a Freshening Breeze

You're out for a day's sail. It's breezing up. You'll need to tighten up your rig to prepare your boat for the oncoming wind. It's time to make adjustments to the running rigging. The sails need to be flattened and their draft moved slightly forward. Among the methods for doing this are luff tensioning, foot tensioning (if the sails have booms), and mast bend. While these techniques are particularly critical for racing sailors, they are also valuable skills for a cruising sailor in a freshening breeze.

Luff tensioning, which may be done with the halyard or downhaul, is particularly effective, because it both flattens the sail and moves the draft forward. The draft curve tends to move aft in a fresh breeze, and this not only increases drag, but also produces extra side force, which increases heeling. Thus, it is essential to keep the luff tight as the wind freshens. The degree of tightness depends mainly on the stability of your sails. Soft cloth with little or no filler may require continual tightening with a lot of tension in the strongest breeze, but a heavily resinated sail, or especially one of Mylar, should not be tightened much more than necessary to remove small horizontal wrinkles along the luff. A downhaul used for luff tensioning is usually a line or tackle that pulls down on the tack or on a grommet a foot or so above the tack, called a Cunningham cringle. The latter allows the luff to be tensioned when there is a fixed boom or a black band on the mast to limit luff length for the most favorable rating under handicap racing rules. The

83

band is normally used when the boom's gooseneck can slide up
or down on a mast track (see the accompanying illustration).

Foot tensioning, which flattens the lower part of a boomed
sail, is achieved with an outhaul or flattening reef. The outhaul
usually takes the form of a tackle, worm screw, or crank that
pulls the clew aft. A flattening reef normally is used when foot
tension is limited by a black band (for rating purposes) or when
there simply is no room to stretch out the foot. A line from the
end of the boom is led through a cringle in the leech a short
distance above the clew and then through a cheek block at the
boom's end and forward to a winch (see illustration). This
provides more room for outhauling to tighten the foot and also
slightly reduces the sail area. Another benefit of this type of
flattening reef is that it lifts the end of the boom slightly,
thereby safeguarding against tripping when sailing on a broad
reach or run in a seaway that causes the boat to roll severely.

Another technique—used primarily by racers but viable
nonetheless—is mast bend, a means of flattening the mainsail.
The head of the mast is pulled aft while its middle is bowed
forward, thereby flattening the draft curves near the middle of

A tack band and Cunningham.

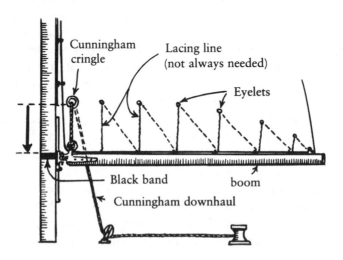

the sail. Sailors of small catboats with flexible rigs merely use sheet and boom vang tension to bend their masts, but tension on a permanent backstay is the principal means for inducing bend on most racing sloops.

Just how much bend you use will depend on the degree of flexibility in the rig, the cut of the mainsail, and the design of the rig (masthead or fractional). The rig's flexibility has to do with such factors as the sectional size of the mast, the standing rigging plan, and the position of the spreaders. If you have a one-design boat, find out the degree of mast bend used by sister

Flattening reef.

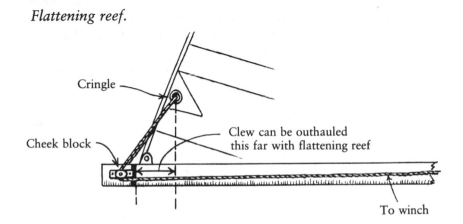

Cringle

Cheek block

Clew can be outhauled this far with flattening reef

To winch

Mast bend.

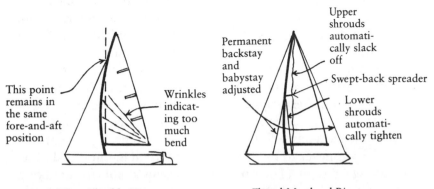

This point remains in the same fore-and-aft position

Wrinkles indicating too much bend

Permanent backstay and babystay adjusted

Upper shrouds automatically slack off

Swept-back spreader

Lower shrouds automatically tighten

Flexible Rig

Flexed Masthead Rig

boats and/or discuss the matter with a sailmaker. Sails must be cut for a given amount of mast bend. One sign that you are bending the mast too much is the formation of prominent wrinkles running from the clew to the middle of the luff, as illustrated.

As a general rule, boats with jibstays that run to the mast-head use relatively little bend compared to boats with fractional rigs. A conservative rule for flexing the average mast having a headstay is to move the luff forward a distance of one-half the fore-and-aft sectional dimension of the mast. Fractional rigs are flexed to a greater degree, because the jibstay acts as a fulcrum and minimizes compression loading, which weakens the mast. Also, mainsail shaping is more important on a fractionally rigged boat, since that sail is larger than the jib. The mast of a masthead-rigged boat usually is bent by tightening the backstay against taut forward lower shrouds or a baby stay, which leads from midmast to the middle of the foredeck.

One governing factor in bending any mast is the ability to keep the jibstay taut for windward work. On a fractionally rigged boat, the mast must curve aft above the point where the stay attaches to the mast and curve forward below that point in order to keep the stay taut. A slack jibstay is harmful in a fresh breeze, because it increases the jib's draft and turns it more to the side, thereby increasing heeling and reducing thrust and pointing ability. To ensure proper jibstay tension, most fractional rigs need running backstays that attach to the mast very close to the point where the jibstay attaches. In this location, they can directly oppose the jib's forward pull. Runners also help steady the mast and keep it from pumping in a seaway. Even some masthead rigs may need runners if the mast tends to pump a great deal. The usual means of keeping the headstay taut on a masthead-rigged boat is to tension the permanent backstay, which directly opposes the headstay. If you have a hydraulic backstay adjuster with tension gauge, a prudent rule to follow is never to tighten the stay more than one-third of its breaking strength. (The Appendix contains a table for breaking strengths of 1 x 19 stainless steel wire, the most commonly used low-stretch rigging wire.)

If the wind continues to increase after you have flattened your sails, you need to change their trim. Particularly if you are sailing to windward, ease the mainsheet traveler (if you have one) so that the lead moves to leeward. Doing so may cause the mainsail to bulge or luff slightly just abaft the mast, but this does little harm and will reduce heeling and the excessive weather helm caused by it. The net effect is beneficial. Jibs with inboard leads should be led to the rail—a change comparable to shifting a traveler to leeward. As the wind continues to freshen, you might want to move the jib lead block slightly farther aft to open the leech and allow the sail to spill some wind to reduce heeling. An exception to this rule might be when the leech is motorboating, despite a taut leech line. When there is a small jib set in a very strong wind, it is best to keep the lead fairly far forward to reduce motorboating and increase the small jib's power with a bit more camber to help power through choppy seas.

Although what I have suggested may seem somewhat contradictory, it is important to make a distinction between sailing in heavy winds in relatively unchoppy waters and sailing in somewhat lighter winds in shorter, steeper waves (often produced by shoal water or a strong current against the wind). In the latter case, you want a bit more draft and perhaps slightly larger sails to move you through the seas. If you lack power when sailing upwind, choppy seas can stop you dead. Even if you are not trying to sail fast, you need enough speed to gain good steerageway and to prevent the possibility of getting caught in stays with your sails aback. But remember: Do not overdo the amount of camber, and keep the draft fairly far forward, with ample luff tension.

The boom vang, normally a tackle but sometimes a lever or rod hydraulically operated, is an important piece of gear, because it controls the twist in a boomed sail. To minimize twist in a fresh breeze, it usually should be tight. This is especially important when broad reaching or running in a blow, because a severely twisted sail will have its upper part more broad off than its lower part, and the upper draft curves may produce thrust that is directed slightly to windward (see illustration). In this case, the boat is more prone to yawing, and especially to rolling.

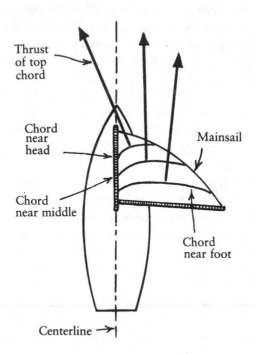

Thrust
of top
chord

Chord
near
head

Mainsail

Chord
near middle

Chord
near foot

Centerline

Sail twist when running.

There are two basic ways to rig the vang. An on-center vang runs from the bottom of the boom (several feet away from the mast) down to the base of the mast; an off-center vang is rigged from the same point on the boom to the side deck or rail. The on-center vang will hold the boom down securely during a jibe and thus avoid a Chinese (or goosewing) jibe (when the boom lifts and swings across the boat while the upper part of the sail remains on the original side). The off-center vang has to be removed when jibing, and it must be adjusted continually when the sail's trim is changed. It has the advantage, however, of acting as a preventer, holding the boom stationary in the event of an accidental jibe.

When running before steep seas, I prefer either an off-center vang or an on-center vang with a preventer (in the form of a line running from the boom's end to some secure point on the foredeck). If you do not rig a preventer, don't sail dead before the wind when the boat is yawing. The tail of an off-center vang tackle should be led back to the cockpit, as shown in the photograph, so that the vang can be released immediately in the event of a severe roll that submerges the boom's end. To guard against tripping and possibly breaking the boom in extreme conditions, use the flattening reef (described earlier) to raise the boom's end.

While on the subject of running in strong winds, I suggest winging out your working sails to achieve balance. When all your sails are on one side of the boat, steering often is more

An off-center vang, rigged to the side deck, requires adjustments when the sail's trim is changed; but it has the advantage of acting as a preventer, holding the boom stationary in the event of an accidental jibe.

difficult, and the after sail will blanket any sail farther forward. Multimast boats can sail wing-and-wing—for instance, a schooner can carry her main on one side and her foresail on the other, while a ketch can carry her mizzen opposite her main.

A sloop or cutter can wing out her jib with or without a pole. In the latter case, it is easiest first to trim an overlapping jib to a point where its clew is just about opposite the forward or upper shroud (depending on the jib's overlap), and then jibe the main, allowing the jib to remain as it is. Head dead downwind to keep the jib full, but here again, rig a preventer on the main boom to avert an accidental jibe.

It is safer to pole out the jib so that you can sail a bit higher than dead downwind. The simplest method of poling out a jib is to set up your spinnaker pole on the windward side, keeping the jib blanketed in the lee of the main, and then outhaul the jib's clew to the outboard end of the pole. The outhauling is done with the jib's windward sheet, which is run through the pole's end fitting. The pole is held up with a topping lift, and in very strong winds you may want guys to control its fore-and-aft swing.

I won't say much about the spinnaker. No less a seaman than Sir Francis Chichester called it "a lubberly sail." At the very least, it is a sail that can cause plenty of trouble in windy weather unless you have a crew well practiced and thoroughly experienced in spinnaker handling. On competitive offshore racers, small, heavy spinnakers with narrow shoulders are sometimes carried when running in up to moderate gale conditions; but when the wind is abeam, the sail is apt to invite repeated broaching. Sound seamanship argues against carrying a spinnaker whenever the risk of severe or repeated broaching exists, especially when there are steep seas.

If you are determined to fly the 'chute (spinnaker) in a blow, the following suggestions may be of some benefit:

• Become accomplished using the spinnaker in light airs before using it in fresh winds.
• In a breeze, hoist the 'chute and hand it in the lee of the mainsail. In very strong winds, stop the sail with light

twine that can be broken with a hard tug on the sheet or a breaking line after the sail is hoisted.

• Bear in mind that even a fairly lightweight 'chute can be carried in heavy winds when running, but it can cause a leeward knockdown that will lead to broaching when reaching.

• At the first sign of a broach—heralded by a strong gust and consequent heeling to leeward—bear off immediately to gain stability, but don't bear off to a dead run in steep seas, as a yaw could cause an inadvertent jibe.

• If the rudder starts to stall or lose its effectiveness, release the spinnaker sheet and slack off the boom vang.

• To prevent a windward knockdown while running, guy the pole farther forward, trim the sheet, and head up—the opposite of what you would do to avoid a leeward knockdown.

Spinnaker in trouble in a blow. Attempting to fly the 'chute in heavy conditions with the wind abeam is apt to invite repeated broaching. (Karina Paape photo)

• When the spinnaker is oscillating and the boat rolling on a run, do your best to flatten the sail and stabilize it. This often means tightening the halyard, overtrimming the sheet and leading it farther forward, and keeping the pole reasonably low.

• When jibing in a blow, use the dip-pole method (dipping the end of the pole under the forestay), and use double guys and sheets for better control. The double lines also mean that you can get plenty of slack for easy insertion of the new guy into the pole's end fitting.

• In rough seas, especially offshore, use a spinnaker net, or "phantom jib," which fills in the foretriangle area with lines or tapes to prevent the 'chute from wrapping itself around the forestay.

A more seamanlike rig than the spinnaker for running in a cruising boat during windy weather is the "wung out" jib already discussed. If you want to sail almost as fast as a boat carrying a spinnaker but with better balance, try double headsails. *Kelpie* has had a lot of success in nonspinnaker races carrying (in addition to her main) a large reaching jib having a wire luff, set flying (unhanked) opposite a poled-out genoa. We have used this rig with excellent steering control in winds up to 40 knots, when spinnaker-carrying boats near us were broaching repeatedly. In light airs, we once overtook close aboard a fractional-rigged Southern Ocean Racing Circuit (SORC) champion that was carrying a spinnaker, because our double jibs had more projected area.

The secret of using this combination is to rig your boomed-out jib so that it spills its wind into the other jib, which ordinarily would be blanketed by the mainsail (see illustration). On *Kelpie,* this requires running the pole between the forward and upper shrouds. If using this rig while racing, be sure to check its legality in your class rules.

When reaching with the wind nearly on the beam, move your jib lead farther forward to prevent excessive headsail twist. It is best to carry a reaching jib, which is cut with a high clew to minimize twist. Another benefit of the high clew is that

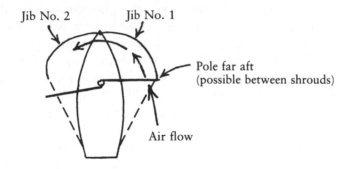

Winged double jibs.

it keeps the sail's foot clear of the bow wave. If you plan to reach with a low-foot genoa, have a grommet installed near the middle of the foot so that you can use a spare halyard or pole lift to lift it clear of the bow wave. It's a good idea to use a short length of shock cord between the foot grommet and halyard shackle to reduce shock loading if a sea should hit the sail.

Reducing Sail

Now let's suppose that the wind continues to freshen, and despite the aforementioned changes in trim and sail shaping adjustments, the boat is being overpowered; the rail is being submerged and steering is becoming difficult. The time has come to shorten down or reduce sail through sail removal, changes, reefing, or some combination of these.

Every boat has a heeling angle beyond which performance begins to decline, and when that angle is reached, sail reduction should begin. The transition heeling angle, where optimal performance starts to deteriorate, varies with different boats. A beamy racer with fine bow and full stern may have a transition angle of around 15 degrees, whereas a narrower and more symmetrical hull with long overhangs may still perform well when she is heeled to 25 degrees or more, largely as a result of her balanced hull and increased sailing length when heeled. However, it is unwise to sail any boat with her rail buried.

Chapter 3 began the discussion of reduced sail plans and basic reefing systems as well as the importance of helm balance and sail concentration. Here, I would like to make a few suggestions on the technique of shortening down, paying particular concern to safety and the curtailment of effort.

First, let me urge care and deliberation in going forward to handle sails in a seaway. Move with caution along the windward side deck and use the grabrails and/or lifelines for security and balance. Someone in the cockpit should be ready to call out a warning to the foredeck crew when he sees that a particularly steep, breaking wave is about to strike the boat. When working forward, keep your weight low and your feet wide apart; kneel when handing jibs. In rough waters, use your safety harness. Nets rigged between the lifelines and the toe-rails on each side of the foredeck are a great help.

When there is a sudden freshening of the wind, some sailors simply drop the mainsail and sail under a large headsail (perhaps a No. 1 genoa), but this can be a dangerous practice in rough seas, as the mast then comes under considerable strain, with all the load at its top and no mainsail to support its middle. When you want to drop one sail quickly, it usually is safer to drop the jib and leave the mainsail hoisted. Dropping the jib makes sense when you are hit by a sudden squall but not for prolonged sailing, because the boat will suffer from loss of balance and power, especially if she has a small mainsail.

In a gradually freshening wind, when you have plenty of warning that it's breezing up, set a medium-sized jib early. Don't replace the No. 1 genoa with a small jib, because this may cause you to lose too much power. With the medium jib, another headsail change might not be necessary, because the next step in shortening down is reefing the main. This is relatively easy, and the boat will maintain good balance as the center of effort moves slightly forward to counteract the extra weather helm caused by heeling. The medium jib should have a long luff to provide good thrust and little if any overlap. A high-cut foot will help keep it clear of the seas. Despite having a fairly high center of effort, this jib should not cause excessive heeling, since most of its thrust will be directed ahead rather than abeam.

If a real blow should develop, of course—Force 7 or above—you will need a small jib. To make the change, I suggest the following procedure when beating and when you don't want to lose distance to windward. Assuming that you have hank-on jibs, plan to make the change while coming about. Prior to changing, hank on the replacement jib under the one that's flying. To do this, you need double tack snapshackles or hooks, so that both sails can be tacked down simultaneously. Lay out the replacement jib's sheets on the windward side, and properly position its lead block. When all is ready, the helmsman tacks, turning slowly through the eye of the wind. Meanwhile, lower the standing jib and unhank it as it comes down. Transfer the halyard to the replacement, and hoist away as soon as you fill away on the new tack. When you leave the hanked-on replacement jib on deck for any length of time, be sure it is well stopped. A good trick is to stop it to the lifeline (see photograph), where it will be clear of the bow wave.

When you have plenty of searoom to leeward and are not racing or concerned about losing distance to windward, you can greatly simplify a headsail change by bearing off almost to a dead run before changing. Doing so reduces the motion, levels the deck, creates a partial lee behind the mainsail, and reduces the apparent wind so that sails can be handled more easily.

Whatever changing system you use, be sure the halyards are clear to run and their ends are knotted through cleats or otherwise secured to prevent them from going aloft. Never leave an unstopped sail on deck, and be sure its tack is always connected to the tack fitting. Carry an extra stop in your pocket in case the jib needs further subduing. To simplify lowering and holding the jib down, rig a downhaul leading from the jib's head to a block near the tack and then aft. The downhaul will further muzzle the sail if it is run from the head to a

Adlard Coles, author of Heavy Weather Sailing, *at the helm of his double-ender* Cohoe. *Notice the furled jib hanked on under the genoa and stopped to the lower lifeline. This greatly facilitates headsail changing. (Beken photo)*

ring seized to a hank lower than midway up the luff, and then through the clew grommet and forward to the tack block, as shown in the illustration. This rig, sometimes called a Gerr downhaul, will pull the clew forward if the sheet is released as the sail comes down.

When it comes time to clap in a reef, consider the following tips:

- Be sure the sail's sheet is well eased before it is reefed, as taking pressure off the sail makes the job much easier.
- If you have jiffy, or slab, reefing, mark the halyard with tape, twine, and/or paint that will line up with a mark on the

A slight variation of a Gerr downhaul.

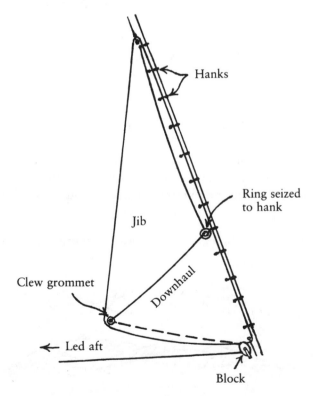

mast to show the amount of slack needed to attach the tack grommet to its hook at the gooseneck. Be sure the topping lift is taut before lowering the sail.

- If your sail has slides that attach it to the boom, pass the reef points between the sail's boltrope and the boom. Never tie the points around the boom, since the tension on each point will vary, and the sail could be damaged.
- The reverse surgeon's knot, as shown in the illustration, is more efficient than the traditional square knot for tying reef points.
- When your sail's foot is held down by a boltrope that fits into a groove on the boom, use one long lacing line that runs through reefing eyelets and spirals around the boom.
- With jiffy reefing, it is a good idea to put a gasket (short line) through the clew cringle and around the boom. This safeguards against a torn sail if someone should slack the clew earing before the points are untied.
- With roller reefing, install a few grommets in the sail's leech at positions where you would usually want to reef. With these, you can rig an outhaul to improve the shape of the reefed sail.
- To prevent boom-end droop with roller reefing, fasten wedge-shaped wood strips to your boom to increase its diameter at the after end.
- When your boom slides up and down on a mast track, you can simplify a shallow roller reef by allowing the boom to slide upward to the top of the track as you rotate the boom.

The reverse surgeon's knot, effective for tying reef points.

• Be sure your lower batten is parallel with the boom so that it won't be bent when it is rolled snug against the boom.

• If you have a roller-furling jib, be sure that its stay or foil is taut, as this helps flatten the sail and facilitates rolling the sail to reef it in a strong wind.

• If you plan to sail with your jib partially furled, have the jib cut fairly flat. Consider using a system that reduces camber as the sail is rolled, such as North Sails' Aeroluff system (a rotating boltrope in the middle of the luff), foam luff (a foam-padded luff), or a double-swivel drum (a drum with double-swivel action, permitting the tack and head to lag slightly behind the foil as it turns).

• At frequently used reef positions, have the roller jib reinforced with patches where the luff and foot bear against the stay or foil.

• Use a sail cut that permits increasing weight of cloth from the luff to the leech, so that the sail becomes increasingly heavy as it is roller reefed.

• For offshore cruising, consider a roller foil that accepts sail slugs, and/or use an inner forestay that can carry a hanked-on staysail.

Before and after sail reduction, be sure to scrutinize the mast and rigging. See that the mast is not unduly bending or pumping. Check the shrouds to see that they are well secured and not excessively slack on the leeward side. A careful seaman glances at the leeward spreaders as well as the shrouds before tacking in a fresh breeze. Also, check for chafe periodically. Are rope halyards or other lines being worn? Is a wire topping lift chafing the leech of any sail? Also, check the sails to see that there are no seams beginning to split, no broken battens, nor anything amiss. In other words, always keep your eyes on the lookout for potential trouble spots.

One final—and probably obvious—word of advice: The drill of sail reduction will go much more smoothly when the time comes if it has first been practiced under less windy conditions.

6

Windy Weather Helmsmanship

Windy-weather sailing poses special challenges for the helmsman. The combination of strong gusts and steep seas can substantially affect a boat's handling characteristics and necessitates certain important modifications of basic sailing technique. This chapter reviews some of the fundamentals of sailing in a breeze.

Dealing with Gusts

When sailing upwind, your weight should be to windward, and in a small centerboarder you will have to hike out to minimize heeling. It is best if your cockpit has hiking straps under which you can hook your feet in order to lean out without falling overboard. On most boats with fine bows and full sterns, the crew weight should be abaft amidships, and it should be concentrated to minimize hobbyhorsing. When hiking far out to windward and sailing into the lee of a ship, bank, or some other large object that blocks the wind, take particular care not to capsize to windward. Also, be sure to shift your weight inboard promptly when tacking or jibing.

If the boat is hit by a strong puff, the usual response is to luff up toward the wind and/or release your sheets to spill wind from the sails. An exception to the luffing rule might occur when you are sailing quite far off the wind on a broad reach. In this case, if you can immediately ease the sheet of the mainsail or after sail, it might be best to bear off to a run, on which point of sailing the boat will be most stable. Should the boat have a strong weather helm, however, and the mainsheet cannot be eased immediately, let the boat come up into the wind. Don't bear off.

The perilous results of bearing off in such a situation were demonstrated not long ago, when a tall ship replica was

The crew of this small centerboarder have their feet under a hiking strap to reduce the risk of falling overboard as they lean out to windward to keep the boat on her feet. (Roger Shope photo)

knocked down by an exceptionally strong gust and lives were lost. Held down by the wind, she could not right, because her helmsman reportedly tried to bear off before the mainsheet could be released. This caused her to lie on her side long enough to fill—primarily through a large, open hatch—and sink. The foundering was caused by her lack of watertight integrity, but it appears that the ship would have had a better chance of surviving had the helmsman allowed her to do what she wanted—weathercock into the wind. I would turn a boat away from the wind in similar circumstances *only* if all or most of the following conditions existed: the point of sailing was definitely below a beam reach; the boat was a fairly light-displacement type that could accelerate rapidly and thus gain stability; the boat had a deep, effective rudder not prone to stalling; the weather helm was moderate or less; and, most important, the mainsheet could be slacked immediately.

In small, capsizable centerboarders, especially, it is important to have a mainsheet that releases easily. Normally, it is held by a cam cleat (see illustration) and tended by the helmsman. When it needs slacking, the helmsman can yank the sheet out of the cleat. Most often, the cam cleat is at the bottom of a sheet tackle, so a downward yank on the sheet releases it. If it is difficult to remove, sometimes you can step on the sheet near the cleat while holding the line in your hand.

On large boats with winches for the mainsheet, double-horn jam cleats can be used, but take care not to mount them

Cam-action jam cleats, commonly known as cam cleats.

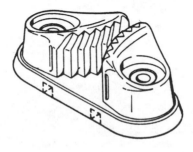

so that they are aligned exactly in the direction of the sheet's pull. This type of cleat should be aligned so that its axis is 15 to 30 degrees away from the direction of the line. When the angle is less than 15 degrees, the line could be overly jammed so that it cannot be released immediately. Other alternatives are self-tailing winches with their own integral cleats and clam cleats mounted near the winch. The latter are nonmoving jams (see accompanying photograph) that allow relatively easy removal of the sheet.

Easily capsizable boats, such as certain multihulls, ought to have automatic sheet releases. These can be complicated mercury switch releases that act when the boat reaches a certain angle of heel; or they can be simple hinged cam cleats, which use a thumb screw to adjust the pressure required for the cleat to flip up and release.

When beating to windward, you need to luff up rather than ease the sheet. Ease only in an emergency, when you are in danger of a severe knockdown. Luffing up not only will spill the wind from the sail for greater stability, but also allow you to make more distance upwind. When I say "ease," I mean "start," or slack off a considerable amount; it may be highly desirable to "crack" your sheet (ease only a small amount) in order to get more power to punch through the seas. The technique of luffing up while beating to windward is called "feathering."

A clam cleat. (Sally Henderson photo)

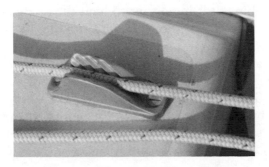

The so-called fisherman's reef consists of carrying a trimmed-in headsail with a pronounced luff in the mainsail. This is acceptable practice for short periods or time, but beware of allowing the mainsail to shake for a long time, as this can be very hard on the sail. The fisherman's reef is most appropriate when the wind is puffy and sail reduction would mean that the boat would be underpowered a large part of the time.

A final important point about dealing with gusts is that when you are beating in very strong puffs which threaten to capsize and you must ease sheets, you should usually ease the jib as well as the mainsail to maintain proper balance. If you ease the main only and leave the jib trimmed flat, you may lack sufficient weather helm to allow a rapid turn toward the wind if such a maneuver should become necessary to avert a capsize.

Getting Her About

When it is necessary or desirable to change tacks, tacking usually is safer than jibing. However, in steep breaking seas, tacking may be out of the question for small, light-displacement boats or sluggish, reefed-down heavy craft. (Deep reefing has its liabilities, since it hinders the boat's ability to get about.) In such instances, it may be best—or, in fact, necessary—to jibe.

When properly executed, the jibing procedure generally is safe and seamanlike. First, wait for a lull in the breeze (if you can), and then try to position your boat in the trough between two seas.

Before jibing, it is important to haul the mainsheet almost all the way in, to reduce shock loading and the risk of the sheet fouling as well as to prevent the boom from riding up. A taut, on-center vang also will hold down the boom. Bear off to a run while quickly trimming in the mainsheet until the boom is amidships. Then turn slightly so that you are sailing by the lee and let the boom swing over. Brace yourself to receive a sudden pull as the sail fills on the other tack, and immediately let the sheet run out until the boom almost touches the after shrouds.

The helmsman holds the boat off to a run on the new tack until everything is under control. The boat should not be rounded up immediately after the jibe, as this could lead to a broach, with the centrifugal force from the run reinforcing the wind's heeling force. Then, if the boat is hit by a beam sea, she could be rolled over or knocked down. If she is a centerboarder, pull the board about halfway up. This will allow steering control yet reduce the heeling moment.

If the mainsail is too much to handle and cannot be hauled in sufficiently, reef down or lower it before jibing. To keep the sail from fouling the rigging, steer the boat up close to the wind before lowering.

When it is possible to tack without getting in stays and drifting backward, thus increasing vulnerability to knockdowns, try the following technique to help ensure rapid tacking: Wait for a "smooth" (relatively smoother seas), crack off just a bit to get the boat really moving, and then turn her firmly into the wind. Don't jam the helm hard over, but turn her rapidly. Keep the jib full until it breaks (luffs). As the boat comes head-to-wind, keep the new windward jibsheet tight so that the sail will come aback on the new tack and force the bow to fall off. If the seas stop the boat more than you anticipate, haul in on the windward sheet to back the jib further. After the bow begins to fall off, slack the windward sheet and slowly haul in the leeward sheet. You may want to trim in the mainsail as you round up into the wind, easing it out again when you bear off on the new tack, and then trimming in just a bit after the boat regains her speed.

────────── Keeping a Weather Eye

In windy weather, the helmsman must be on the lookout for strong gusts and steep seas. When sailing to windward, he should sit on the weather side of the boat so that he can scrutinize the water to windward. Of course, as we have seen already, this is especially important in a small centerboarder, as all possible weight is needed on the high side for maximum stability, and the helmsman must be alert to any gust that could cause a knockdown and possible capsize. But even on a large keelboat, the person who steers must be able to see what is coming, for failure to anticipate a gust could cost valuable distance to windward and result in excessive heeling, while a large breaking sea could stop the boat almost dead in her tracks. The helmsman should look for dark patches of ripples on the water surface, indicating an increase in wind velocity and often a change in wind direction. As the boat begins to feel the gust, he should feather to gain distance to windward and prevent excessive heeling. If an oncoming gust is the cat's-paw type that fans out, you will be headed first and then lifted (allowed to head up without the sails luffing). But a puff that strikes the water at a shallow angle without fanning out will lift you immediately, because the increased velocity will draw the apparent wind farther aft (see accompanying diagram).

In addition to studying the water to windward, the helmsman should be looking at his jib luff. Every jib should have

Luff telltales indicate when the sail is stalled or beginning to luff.

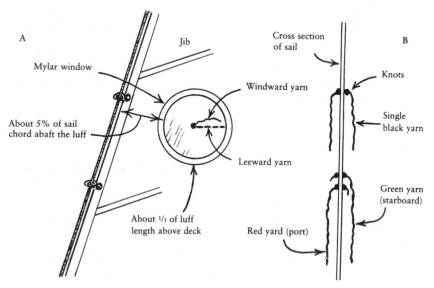

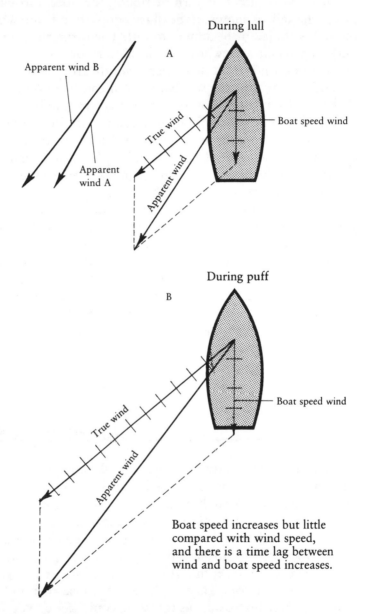

The effect of a puff on apparent wind. Since apparent wind B is farther aft than A, boat B can point higher during the puff.

telltales (short pieces of yarn or ribbon threaded through the luff of the sail, as shown in the illustration) to indicate whether the sail is stalled or beginning to luff. The former condition is indicated when a leeward telltale flutters or twirls, and the latter condition is indicated when a windward telltale flutters. In moderate winds, the windward yarn can be allowed to lift slightly when beating, but in fresh winds with lumpy seas, it is a good idea to keep both telltales streaming aft. In other words, keep the boat footing unless you need to luff up to meet or avoid a breaking wave. To see the jib's luff, the helmsman must sit far to windward; this usually requires a tiller extension or large-diameter wheel.

If you have a knotmeter, check it from time to time. Note your top speed when you are sailing full-and-by (with sails well filled) between seas; when you are slowed by a wave, see how quickly you can get the boat up to top speed again. After being slowed, bear off far enough to get the boat moving but not so far as to lose valuable distance to windward. The exact technique will depend on the particular boat and the type of seas, but whatever the conditions, frequent reference to a knotmeter as well as the compass can be helpful.

Handling a Sea

The technique of steering through seas depends partly on the size and shape of the individual waves. In relatively small waves, you may want to head up when approaching a crest and then momentarily bear off as you are hit by the crest to lessen impact. When there are steep plunging breakers, however, you need to foot off a bit to gain speed while climbing the face, luff up just before you meet the crest, and quickly bear off again as you go over the top. Take a plunger as close to bow-on as possible, never broadside, as the wave could knock you down and even cause a rolldown in the worst conditions. Obviously, you should try to steer a course that avoids the steepest waves.

Quite often these are caused by the intersection of two different wave trains that are not exactly parallel. When you can't avoid a plunger, don't wait too long before beginning to luff, as turning into the crest at the last instant can increase the impact and cause you to "ship it green." Keep the boat moving when you are not actually luffing, as reasonable speed is essential to maneuverability and steering control. If you are in a small centerboarder, watch out for an increase in wind velocity at the crest of a wave.

When sailing downwind, the seas can be beneficial, provided they are not so large that they threaten to cause a broach or poop (break over the stern). In moderate seas, you want to steer dead before the crests and keep the boat flat (unheeled) for maximum benefit from surfing (semiplaning down the face of waves). In steeper seas, however, it may be helpful to take the waves at a slight angle, perhaps 15 to 20 degrees from being square to the wave line, to keep the bow from burying and to

A spinnaker broach. Notice how the rudder has lost its effectiveness. (Karina Paape photo)

avoid any possibility of an accidental jibe. Do not head up too
far, however, because of the danger of a broach. Broaching-to
is potentially hazardous in plunging seas, because an inadvertent rounding up toward the wind exposes the boat to steep
waves with breaking tops on her beam, while the centrifugal
force of a sudden turn can combine with the breakers to cause
a dangerous knockdown or roll-over. Bear in mind that a vessel
is in a position of least stability when she is beam-to the seas,
and remember that a rudder loses its effectiveness when the
boat is well heeled. Never head up so high that there is very
strong pressure on the helm, because this could stall the rudder.

If the boat is yawing, be extra attentive to steering and try
to anticipate the yaws before the boat begins to turn so that you
can "catch" her before momentum develops. When the bow
starts to bury, move your crew weight aft on the windward side.
In plunging breakers, assign someone to look aft to watch for
potentially dangerous approaching waves; steer a weaving
course to avoid them. If you are in a heavy-displacement boat,
slow her down by reducing sail when her own wave system
becomes steep, because it could reinforce the wind waves
enough to create pooping seas. For best steering control, a centerboarder usually should have its board at least halfway down.

If you want to turn from a downwind to an upwind heading, wait for a lull in the wind and a relatively smooth spot to
perform the maneuver. An old wives' tale predicts that a
"smooth" will come after the seventh wave. There is actually
no such regular pattern for wave size, but a smooth will usually
occur periodically. In steep seas, slow down and turn slowly so
as to minimize the centrifugal force. Delay trimming your sails
flat until you are above the position where the seas are abeam.

If You Should Capsize

If you are sailing a centerboarder and should happen to capsize, remember the cardinal rule: *Stay with your boat.* Nearly
all modern centerboarders are fitted with flotation, so they will

keep you afloat. They usually can be righted by the crew, but if not, the crew that sticks with the boat will be safer and more easily found by rescuers.

When a small centerboarder is knocked down and a capsize seems inevitable—even though the sheets have been released and the helm is hard alee—the first action to take is to scramble up over the windward rail and stand on the centerboard. (As I have stressed, it should have been at least partway down.) This may prevent further heeling and avoid a complete capsize, but if not, it probably will prevent the boat from turning turtle after the mast hits the water. Boats without masthead flotation may tend to roll completely over after their mast fills with water, so it is important for at least one person to stay on the centerboard. Some small boats with a lot of flotation can be righted immediately simply by leaning away from the hull while standing on the board and gripping the gunwale or a short line for extra leverage, as shown in the illustration.

When the boat cannot be righted at once, crew members must don life jackets (if they are not already on). If the boat shows any sign of turtling, fasten a PFD or some other flotation

Righting after capsizing.

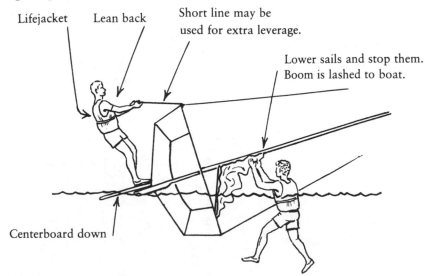

Lifejacket   Lean back   Short line may be used for extra leverage.

Lower sails and stop them. Boom is lashed to boat.

Centerboard down

under the masthead. (Be sure to secure it to the halyard so that it can be pulled down after the boat is righted.) Lower sail, and turn the hull so that it is heading into the wind. Then, with the crew standing on or hauling down on the board from the water, the boat should right. Be sure to steady her as she comes up so that she won't flop over the other way.

The next step is to climb aboard and bail her dry. (Your bucket or other bailer should have been lashed down or stowed in a handy locker so that it couldn't fall overboard.) One crew member should climb over the stern while the others steady the boat. You may want to drop anchor (or set a sea anchor) to keep the boat head-to-wind and improve stability or to prevent her from drifting onto a rocky shore.

If you are approached by a rescue craft, take care that she doesn't bump your boat or foul her prop with floating lines. If possible, right your boat before the rescue craft comes alongside. A capsized boat should never be towed until she has been righted. A swamped boat can be towed slowly a very short distance to make the water flow out over the stern. Then towing should cease until most of the remaining water can be removed by bucket or pump.

Recovery after righting.

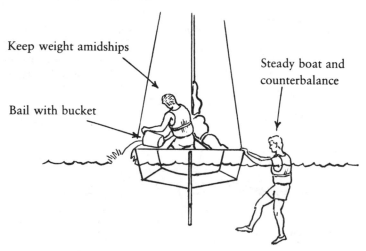

Keep weight amidships

Steady boat and counterbalance

Bail with bucket

In case you are becoming a bit intimidated by the discussion of capsize, remember that capsizing is avoidable. Most such accidents result when racing sailors take chances in the heat of competition. In well over 50 years of sailing, I remember accidentally capsizing only on two occasions, both in my youth, and both resulting from gross carelessness on my part.

One of my capsizes resulted from allowing too much water to accumulate in the bilge. In many boats with minimal flotation, it is important to keep the bilge reasonably dry, because any water taken in from spray, leaks, or rain will run naturally to leeward and detract from the boat's stability. This effect is what naval architects refer to as "free surface." It also can affect (although less drastically) large boats with wide, partially filled tanks. Keel tanks are best for stability because they are deep and narrow, thus less affected by free surface.

My other capsize resulted from waiting too long to lower sail while racing during a squall. A thunderstorm was building, and I, as well as the other racing skippers, had plenty of time to reduce sail, but everyone wanted to delay shortening down until the last possible moment. As a result, we were hit suddenly by a strong cloudburst, and the entire fleet—with one exception—capsized. The exception was a boat handled by two girls, the only pair of females in the fleet, who "chickened out" (or perhaps displayed the best seamanship) and dropped their sails early. Rather humiliating for us boys.

7

Storm Tactics

This is not a book about "heavy weather sailing" in the sense of surviving hurricanes and similar vicious storms at sea. Nonetheless, anyone who does a lot of sailing is apt to get caught out in a hard chance on rare occasions. You might be making a coastal passage when a secondary low suddenly develops along a cold front before it is detected and broadcast by the National Weather Service; or you might be out for a day's sail and be caught by a fast-developing, isolated thunderstorm. In either case—or in any other kind of sudden-storm situation—you should know your tactical options.

Here are the storm tactics:

- Continue sailing with storm sails or greatly reduced working sails.
- Use the engine with or without sails.
- Anchor in shallow waters or use a sea anchor offshore.
- Heave-to under reduced sail.
- Lie ahull under bare poles.
- Run off under greatly reduced sail or bare poles (also known as "scudding").

The first option listed may be the most practical plan when you have a seaworthy boat with an efficient means of reefing down and/or proper storm sails. In fact, making some progress to windward may be essential if you are on a lee shore. Even in a situation where you have plenty of searoom but do not want to lose distance to windward, you can jog slowly to windward against the seas. Do not try to drive into them with great speed if you are not racing, because they will break aboard with considerable force. Keep up enough speed to retain steerageway and to hold the bow up reasonably close to the wind. The sail plan's center of effort should be far enough aft to prevent the bow from being knocked off excessively by breaking seas. If you are reaching toward a destination, be careful not to get broadside to a plunging breaker. Sail a weaving course to avoid dangerous crests and take an unavoidable breaker as close as possible to end-on to minimize the risk of a rollover.

Boats with engines often can use them effectively to augment drive and pointing ability from small sails, or to power directly into the seas without sails. The latter tactic is very often advisable when you are hit by a sudden thunderstorm. (One controversial theory alleges that wet sails can attract lightning.) Quickly drop your sails after turning on the kicker, and use the engine to hold your bow into the waves. In rough waters, use no more power than is necessary to keep the bow up. Heading into the seas may not be the same direction as your destination, but at least thunderstorms seldom last very long.

Anchoring is sometimes desirable when you can tuck up under a windward shore to wait out a thunderstorm. This tactic offers the advantage of better personal protection from lightning because the crew then can go below. If you do stay on deck, never grasp metal rigging or lifelines. Be sure, of course, that your rig is properly grounded so that a lightning strike will cause minimal damage and static charges will bleed off, thereby minimizing the possibility of a dangerous strike.

In deep water, where you can't use a conventional metal anchor, consider using a sea anchor that provides considerable drag, such as the parachute type. Theoretically, this should hold the boat end-to the seas and minimize the risk of a rollover, but most modern yachts behave abominably with the sea anchor streamed from the bow in heavy seas. They tend to strain, jerk, yaw, and spend much of the time beam-to the seas. If the boat has ample freeboard aft, a small self-bailing cockpit, and sturdy companionway slides, consider streaming the sea anchor from the stern. I favor the kind of anchor known as a drogue, which affords some give. It is used mainly as a drag towed astern to slow a boat's speed when she runs before it. More about this in the discussion of running off.

A classic means of riding out a storm is heaving-to. For this tactic, you need a couple of small, counteracting sails. The larger one should be trimmed flat, driving you ahead, and the other should be backed to reduce speed. In the case of a small sloop, the driver would be a deeply reefed main or a storm trysail, and the counteracting sail would be a small headsail such as a spitfire trimmed to windward, as shown in the illustration. When the boat has a large foretriangle or is cutter rigged, a storm staysail would be better than a jib, for reasons discussed in chapter 3.

Heaving-to under sail.

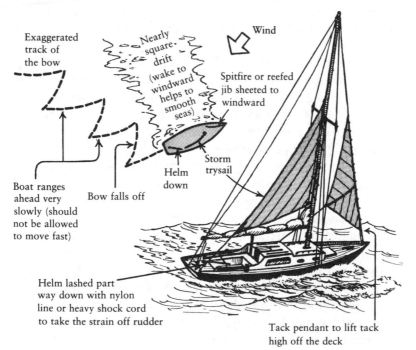

The objects of heaving-to are: (a) to minimize headway so that the boat will not slam or impact violently with the seas; (b) to keep her bow reasonably close to the wind, thereby avoiding steep seas on the beam; (c) to stay fairly fixed in one location when you have little searoom to leeward or don't want to lose much distance to windward; and (d) to make sufficient leeway for a square drift or upwind wake, which helps smooth the seas to weather. The boat's helm is lashed down (rudder to windward) so that she will turn into the wind when driven ahead by the trysail. When she rounds up, the backed headsail causes her to fall off, and the process is repeated so that the bow makes a somewhat zigzag track, as illustrated.

Lying ahull, sometimes referred to as hulling, is a somewhat controversial tactic, but it can be useful under the right circumstances. It probably is the easiest maneuver, because you simply drop all sail, lash the helm alee, and go below, allowing the boat to look after herself. This tactic makes a great deal of sense when the boat has plenty of searoom in a remote area away from traffic and you are shorthanded, perhaps with a sick or exhausted crew. The danger of this plan is that the boat will lie nearly beam-to the seas and you risk rolling over or having a heavy sea dump on the cabintop.

We have lain ahull overnight twice in *Kelpie* during gales at sea, and we were very comfortable, but I would not use the tactic if the boat did not have a very high range of stability and a high-crowned (well-curved), strongly braced cabin trunk with small windows. Then, too, I would consider the tactic risky when the waves were predominantly steep plunging breakers—those produced, for example, by a windshift, shoal water, or a wind against a strong current. When lying ahull, at least one person should be on watch to act as a lookout. Also, it is essential to have all gear below well secured; the offwatch crew should be fastened in their bunks in the event of a roll-down.

Running off under little or no sail is also controversial. A necessary requirement is sufficient headway for the rudder to provide good steering control, but some sailors believe in running at high speed and others at low speed, towing drags. In fact, the proper speed depends on the kind of sea faced and, to a great extent, on crew ability and boat type. In short, steep seas, a heavy-displacement boat should not be driven down-wind so fast that her stern wave reinforces the following seas, as this could cause pooping breakers, especially if the boat has a tendency to squat (depress her stern). On the other hand, a light-displacement boat with buoyant stern and good steering control might be driven with considerable speed and be able to dodge any breakers—*provided* she has skillful and alert helms-men. However, certain modern yachts with very fine bows and a tendency to yaw should only be driven downwind at moder-ate speeds in steep seas, for at faster speeds they run the risk of broaching-to.

Speed may be slowed by towing heavy lines, preferably in a bight, or loop, with or without drags attached. This will hamper steering, but less so if the lines are attached at each side amidships rather than at the stern. You can buy a nautical drogue specifically designed for the purpose, but weighted au-tomobile tires also make effective drags. I have even heard of one instance in which an 18-footer successfully rode out a Force 10 gale using a 15-pound mushroom anchor for a drag. A highly touted drogue is the Galerider, made by the sailmak-ing firm Hathaway, Reiser, and Raymond. Its parabolic shape and open web construction apparently minimize shock loading while allowing reasonable steering control. When yawing is a problem, a very small jib set forward and sheeted flat may help hold off the bow.

The tactic you decide to use, of course, will depend on the particular conditions. Some of the factors to take into consider-ation are: the anticipated severity and duration of the storm, the suitability of your boat for the various tactics, the ability of your crew, and your location with regard to exposure and sea-room. It can be a great temptation to make for a protected harbor when the weather deteriorates, but it also can be risky to try to enter a harbor in the teeth of a blow when it is on a lee shore and visibility is impaired. Often the safer alternative is to head away from the shore to gain adequate searoom. On the other hand, you can consider entering a harbor if it is on a

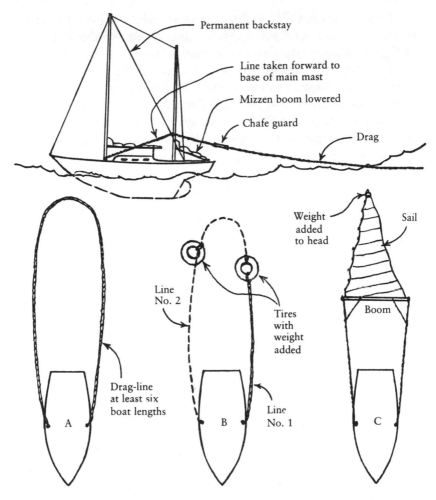

Towing drags. Attaching the drag line to the mizzenmast, as illustrated, will improve steering control. A towed sail can also be an effective drag, but if the boom is attached as illustrated, be sure that it is towed far astern.

windward shore and well marked with navigation aids, if your boat is manageable, and if you are sure the harbor will afford good protection even if the wind shifts.

I hope this brief discussion of storm tactics has been helpful to those of you who are apprehensive about windy-weather sailing. It is comforting to know that unless you are making a long passage offshore, most bad weather can be avoided; and if you should happen to be caught by a fast-developing squall, such as an isolated air-mass thunderstorm, it will most likely dissipate or blow over almost as quickly as it materializes. With a seaworthy boat and proper seamanship, you should be able to ride it out successfully.

Appendix
Mast and Rigging Strength

Any skipper who sails offshore would be well advised to check the strength of his rigging and mast. A simple formula for rigging size is

$$Pt = \frac{RM_{30} \times 1.5}{\frac{1}{2} \text{ beam}}$$

where Pt is the load in pounds on a chainplate from the transverse rigging (shrouds). RM_{30} is the righting moment at 30 degrees of heel, and this may be obtained from the rating certificate of your boat or a sister boat. Most measurement handicap certificates, needed for racing, give the righting moment for one or two degrees of heel and the RM for 30 degrees can be extrapolated with sufficient accuracy by multiplying RM_1 (or RM_2) by 28. Half beam in the formula is the distance from the chainplates to the boat's centerline. Multiply Pt by a safety factor of at least 2.5. This produces the highest total shroud loading, which then is multiplied by percentages for each shroud. These load percentages, derived from tests, are shown in the accompanying illustration. After figuring the load for each shroud, obtain its breaking strength from a rigging catalog. (See the breaking strength list for 1 x 19 stainless steel wire included with the illustration.) Measure the diameter of your rigging to see that it has breaking strengths equal to or greater than the loads calculated. Headstays and backstays should have breaking strengths at least equal to those of the upper shrouds. If you don't have a stock boat, and she is not measured for racing, her righting moment can be determined by a simple inclining test that can be performed by a local yacht measurer or naval architect. You can even make the test yourself by following instructions in most books on yacht design. Or use the simplified method presented in my book *Understanding Rigs and Rigging*.

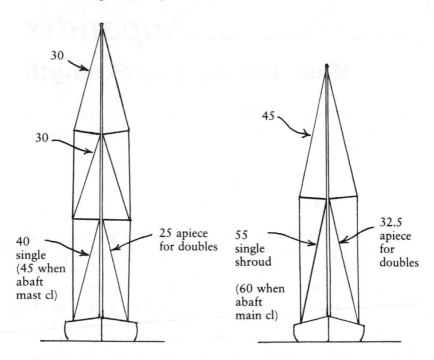

Percentage of total shroud load.

Breaking Strength of 1 x 19 s.s. wire

Diam. (inches)	Load (pounds)
1/8	2100
5/32	3300
3/16	4700
7/32	6300
1/4	8200
9/32	10300
5/16	12500
3/8	17500
7/16	23400
1/2	29700
5/8	46800
3/4	59700

The screening formula for mast strength is a bit more complicated, but I will include a simplified version here, with minimal explanation. (More detail appears in *Understanding Rigs and Rigging.*) Actually, there are two closely related formulas, one for the longitudinal (or fore-and-aft) mast strength and the other for transverse (or lateral) mast strength. They are:

$$\frac{\text{SL} \times 40 \, \text{RM}_1 \times \text{HL}^2}{\text{F} \times \frac{1}{2}\text{B} \times 9.87 \times \text{E}} = \text{longitudinal strength}$$

$$\frac{\text{ST} \times 40 \, \text{RM}_1 \times \text{HT}^2}{\text{F} \times \frac{1}{2}\text{B} \times 9.87 \times \text{E}} = \text{transverse strength}$$

SL is a longitudinal safety factor, which is 2 if the boat has no inner forestay and 1.5 if there is such a stay backed by running backstays. ST is the transverse safety factor, which is 1.7 if the boat has a single-spreader rig and 2 for a double-spreader rig. (Single-spreader rigs need an HT/HL* ratio greater than .5 and spreader length at least .8 times half-beam; double-spreader rigs need an HT/HL ratio greater than .36 and an upper spreader length greater than .6 times half-beam.) RM_1 is the righting moment for one degree of heel, obtainable from the yacht's rating certificate (use RM_2 if the boat has an IMS rating). HL is the mast height in inches above the deck, while HT is the length in inches of the unsupported mast panel between the deck and lower spreaders. F stands for end fixity, which gives a value of 2 when the mast is keel stepped, but only 1.5 if it is deck stepped. B is half beam, the distance in feet from chainplates to the boat's centerline. E is the modulus of elasticity of the mast material, and it is 10,000,000 (pounds per square inch) for aluminum and 1,400,000 for spruce.

Answers to these formulas give moments of inertia expressed in inches to the fourth power. These figures can then be compared with inertia figures given in your sparmaker's sec-

---

* HT = height, transverse; HL = height, longitudinal.

tion data sheets or catalog. Measure the longitudinal and transverse diameters and wall thickness of your mast and look up the section's inertias in the sparmaker's catalog. The actual inertias should be the same or greater then those calculated by the formulas.

Recommended Reading List

If you want to continue your heavy weather sailing education, here are some good choices:

Bowditch, Nathaniel. *The American Practical Navigator*. U.S. Government Printing Office, Washington, DC 20402.

Coles, K. Adlard. *Heavy Weather Sailing*. 3rd rev. ed. New York: John DeGraff, 1981.

Henderson, Richard. *Sea Sense*. 2nd ed. Camden, ME: International Marine Publishing Company, 1979.

_____, *Understanding Rigs and Rigging*. International Marine Publishing Company, 1985.

Houghton, David, and Fred Sanders. *Weather at Sea*. Camden, ME: International Marine Publishing Company, 1988.

Jobson, Gary. *Storm Sailing*. New York: Hearst Marine Books, 1983.

Kotsch, W.J. *Weather for the Mariner*. 3rd ed. Annapolis, MD: Naval Institute Press, 1977.

_____, and Richard Henderson. *Heavy Weather Guide.* 2nd ed. Annapolis, MD: Naval Institute Press, 1984.

Robb, Frank. *Handling Small Boats in Heavy Weather.* Woodstock, NY: Beekman Publishers, 1977.

Taylor, Roger. *The Elements of Seamanship.* Camden, ME: International Marine Publishing Company, 1986.

Index

IMS. *See* International Measurement System
Inclining test, 121
Inertia, 123–124; pitching, 48; roll, 33, 48
Initial stability, 33
In stays, 105
International Measurement System, 38
International Yacht Racing Union, 38
Invicta sloop, 77
Isobars, 13, 18
IYRU. *See* International Yacht Racing Union

Jam cleat. *See* Doublehorn jam cleat
Jibing, 88, 104–105
Jibs: blast, 6; phantom, 92; poling out, 90; roller-furling, 55–57, 99; working, 62, 63. *See also* Spitfire
Jiffy reefing, 53, 54–55, 56, 57, 97, 98

Keelboats, 37–38; long, 32, 33; short, 30, 31
Kelpie, 23, 37–40, 63, 64, 65, 81, 92, 117
Ketch rig, 50, 51, 53, 90
Knockdowns, 35
Knotmeter, 108

Lateral resistance, center of, 50–52
Lead, 52
Lead blocks, 69
Lee helm, 50
Lee shore, 21
Lifelines, 43
Lightning strikes, 115
Lines, 69, 102–103
Load percentages, 121, 122
Load waterline length, 52
Lookout, 82, 105–108
Lows, 7, 14
Luffing up, 78, 103
Luff tensioning, 83–84
LWL. *See* Load waterline length
Lying ahull, 114, 117

Mainsail, 62
Mainsheet, 102–103
Marezine, 79
Marine Weather Service Charts (NOAA), 18
Masthead rig, 85, 86
Masts, 65–66; bend in, 83, 84–86, 99; elasticity of, 123; end fixity of, 123; flotation in, 25, 111; panel length of, 66; strength of, 121–124
Measurement Handicap System, 37, 39
Mercury switch release, 103
Metal fatigue, 66–67
Meteorology, 7–18
MHS. *See* Measurement Handicap System
Miter cut, 59, 60
Mooneshine, 80
Morale, 82
Motorboating, 61, 87
Mylar cloth, 83

Navigation, 81
NOAA VHF/FM broadcasts, 18
North Sails' Aeroluff system, 99

O'Day Day Sailer, 28
Offshore cruisers, 31–33
Ohlson 38A, 37. *See also Kelpie*
Outhaul. *See* Flattening reef
Overnighters, 28–30

Pelican hook, 65
Personal flotation devices, 72, 82, 111
PFDs. *See* Personal flotation devices
Phantom jib, 92
Pitching, 43, 47, 48
Plungers, 47, 108–110, 117
Points reefing, 53, 54, 58
Poling out, 90
Pooping, 109, 118
Predicting windy weather, 1–21
Preparations onboard, 79–82
Pressure systems (weather), 7–14
Preventer. *See* Boom preventer